LABS YOU CAN EAT

HOLT, RINEHART AND WINSTON

A Harcourt Classroom Education Company

Austin • New York • Orlando • Atlanta • San Francisco • Boston • Dallas • Toronto • London

To the Teacher

Would you like your students to really sink their teeth into a scientific concept? If so, the lab activities in this booklet are just what you need! When students know their efforts in the lab will be rewarded with a tasty treat, they are far more likely to become engaged and remain engaged in the investigation of important scientific concepts. This collection of lab activities safely incorporates edible items into the classroom to provide a powerful hands-on, inquiry-based learning tool.

The labs in this booklet are organized into the following three sections—Life Science, Earth Science, and Physical Science. Each lab includes the following:

- **TEACHER'S PREPARATORY GUIDE**
  This guide provides useful information such as the following:

Purpose	Helpful Hints
Time Required	Cooperative Learning Strategies
Lab Ratings	Teaching Strategies
Advance Preparation	Background Information
Safety Information	Evaluation Strategies

- **STUDENT WORKSHEETS**
  These blackline masters make it easy for students to follow procedures and record data using an effective scientific method. Icons at the top of every worksheet distinguish the labs as one of the following types: Skill Builder, Discovery Lab, Making Models, or Design Your Own Experiment. At the end of most labs, students are encouraged to process the information they learned by answering one or more Critical Thinking questions. In addition, many labs include a Going Further extension activity to extend student interest and application.

ANSWER KEY

For your convenience, an Answer Key is available in the back of this booklet. The key includes reduced versions of all applicable worksheets, with answers included on each page.

ASSESSMENT

Several labs include a specific checklist or evaluation form for assessment. The *Assessment Checklists & Rubrics* booklet and the *One-Stop Planner CD-ROM* also include assessment checklists and rubrics. The most appropriate of those grading tools are recommended in the Evaluation Strategies of each Teacher's Preparatory Guide. Look for these icons to identify those tools.

CLASSROOM TESTED & APPROVED

You will also notice this icon, which acknowledges the many teachers around the country who helped ensure the safety, accuracy, and enjoyment of these labs for students.

Credits: See page 119.

Printed in the United States of America

ISBN 0-03-054414-9
    9 10   085   05 04 03

▪ CONTENTS ▪

LIFE SCIENCE LABS

EARTH SCIENCE LABS

Labs You Can Eat: Guidelines for Teachers

Incorporating food into the laboratory is fun and effective, but in order to ensure a safe lab experience for you and your students, keep the following precautions in mind:

- Tell students not to eat any food unless you instruct them to do so. Point out that eating in the laboratory is in general a very unsafe practice. Food can be contaminated by dangerous materials and then ingested, possibly causing serious injury. Also, leftovers, food packaging, crumbs, and other food-related items are a hazard in the laboratory.

- Review with students proper procedures for the storage, preparation, and disposal of food in the classroom. For example, perishable food should be stored in the refrigerator when it is not being used. Also, be sure food items are unspoiled before using them in any activity.

- Before beginning any activity involving food, ask students if they have any food allergies. If a student is allergic to a food, substitute another food in its place and instruct the student not to eat or handle the food.

- Be sure students are aware of proper safety procedures. The safety information on pages vi-viii is designed to be handed out to students. Page viii is a short safety contract that students should read, sign, and return to you to verify that they understand proper safety procedures. Additional safety information is available on the *One-Stop Planner CD-ROM*.

- Even though SI units are used in proper scientific procedure, the English system of measurement is used in most recipes. In this booklet, all measurements are given in SI units, and English units are provided in parentheses when necessary. For your convenience, a brief conversion chart is provided below.

- Dry ingredients are normally measured by mass (in grams). In this booklet, however, dry ingredients are measured by volume (in milliliters) to follow most recipes.

Measurement Conversion Chart

English		SI
1 teaspoon	=	5 mL
1 tablespoon	=	15 mL
1 cup = 8 oz; 16 tbsp	=	240 mL
1 pint = 2 cups	=	470 mL
1 quart = 4 cups	=	950 mL
1 gallon = 4 quarts	=	3.8 L

Safety Guidelines and Symbols for Students

Performing scientific investigations in the laboratory is exciting and fun, but it can be dangerous if the proper precautions aren't followed. To make sure that your laboratory experience is both exciting and safe, follow the general guidelines listed below. Also follow your teacher's instructions, and don't take shortcuts! When you have read and understood all of the information in this section, including the Student Safety Contract, sign your name in the designated space on the contract and return the contract to your teacher.

- **GENERAL** Always get your teacher's permission before attempting any laboratory investigation. Before starting a lab, read the procedures carefully, paying attention to safety information and cautionary statements. If you are unsure about what a safety symbol means, look it up here or ask your teacher. If an accident does occur, inform your teacher immediately.

  Know the location of and the procedure for using the nearest fire alarms and any other safety equipment, such as fire blankets and eyewash fountains. Know the fire-evacuation routes established by your school. Never work alone in the laboratory. Walk with care, and keep your work area free from all unnecessary clutter. Extra books, jackets, and materials can interfere with your experiment and your work. Dress appropriately on lab day. Tie back long hair. Certain products, like hair spray, are flammable and should not be worn while working near an open flame. Remove dangling jewelry. Don't wear opened-toed shoes or sandals in the laboratory.

EYE SAFETY Wear approved safety goggles when working with or around chemicals, any mechanical device, or any type of flame or heating device. If any substance gets in your eyes, notify your teacher. If a spill gets on your skin or clothing, rinse it immediately with water and have someone notify your teacher.

SHARP/POINTED OBJECTS Use knives and other sharp instruments with extreme care. Do not cut an object while holding it in your hands. Instead, place it on a suitable work surface for cutting.

 HEAT Wear safety goggles when using a heating device or a flame. Wear oven mitts to avoid burns.

 HAND SAFETY Avoid chemical or heat injuries to your hands by wearing protective gloves or oven mitts. Check the materials list in the lab for the type of hand protection you should wear while performing the experiment.

 CLOTHING PROTECTION Wear an apron to protect your clothing from staining, burning, or corrosion.

ELECTRICITY Be careful with electrical wiring. When using equipment with an electrical cord, do not place the cord where it could cause someone to trip. Do not let cords hang over a table edge in a way that could cause equipment to fall if the cord is accidentally pulled. Do not use equipment with damaged cords. Be sure your hands are dry and that electrical equipment is turned off before plugging it into the outlet. Turn off all equipment when you are finished using it.

CHEMICALS Wear safety goggles when handling potentially dangerous chemicals. Read chemical labels. Wear an apron and latex gloves when working with acids or bases or when told to do so. If a spill gets on your skin or clothing, rinse it off immediately with water for at least five minutes while notifying your teacher. Never touch, taste, or smell a chemical unless your teacher instructs you to do so. Never mix any chemicals unless your teacher instructs you to do so.

ANIMAL SAFETY Handle animals only as directed by your teacher. Always treat animals carefully and with respect. Wash your hands thoroughly after handling any animal.

PLANT SAFETY Wash your hands thoroughly after handling any part of a plant.

GLASSWARE Examine all glassware before using it. Be sure that it is clean and is free of chips and cracks. Report damaged glassware to your teacher. Glass containers used for heating should be made of heat-resistant glass.

CLEANUP Before leaving, clean your work area. Wash glass containers with soap and water. Put away all equipment and supplies. Dispose of all chemicals and other materials as directed by your teacher. Make sure water, gas, burners, and hot plates are turned off. Make sure all electrical equipment is unplugged. Hot plates and other electrical equipment should also be unplugged. Wash hands with soap and water after working in the laboratory. Never take anything from the laboratory without permission from your teacher.

Safety Contract

Carefully read the Student Safety Contract below. Then write your name in the blank, and sign and date the contract.

STUDENT SAFETY CONTRACT

I will

- [ ] read the lab investigation before coming to class.
- [ ] wear protective equipment as directed to protect my eyes, face, hands, and body while conducting activities.
- [ ] follow all instructions given by the teacher.
- [ ] conduct myself in a responsible manner at all times in a laboratory situation.

I, _____ ,

have read and agree to abide by the safety regulations as set forth above, as well as any additional printed instructions provided by my teacher or the school district.

I agree to follow all other written and oral instructions given in class.

Signature:

_____

Date: _____

SAFETY APPROVED CONTRACT

The Scientific Method

The steps that scientists use to answer questions and solve problems are often called the scientific method. The scientific method is not a rigid procedure. Scientists may use all of the steps or just some of the steps. They may even repeat some steps. The goal of a scientific method is to come up with reliable answers and solutions.

Six Steps of a Scientific Method

1. Ask a Question Good questions come from careful **observations.** You make observations by using your senses to gather information. Sometimes you may use instruments, such as microscopes and telescopes, to extend the range of your senses. As you observe the natural world, you will discover that you have many more questions than answers. These questions drive the scientific method.

Questions beginning with *what, why, how,* and *when* are very important in focusing an investigation, and they often lead to a hypothesis. (You will learn what a hypothesis is in the next step.) Here is an example of a question that could lead to further investigation.

Question: How does acid rain affect plant growth?

2. Form a Hypothesis After you come up with a question, you need to turn the question into a hypothesis. A **hypothesis** is a clear statement of what you expect the answer to your question to be. Your hypothesis will represent your best "educated guess" based on your observations and what you already know. A good hypothesis is one that is testable. If observations and information cannot be gathered or if an experiment cannot be designed to test your hypothesis, it is untestable, and the investigation can go no further.

Here is a hypothesis that could be formed from the question, "How does acid rain affect plant growth?"

Hypothesis: Acid rain causes plants to grow more slowly.

Notice that the hypothesis provides some specifics that lead to methods of testing. The hypothesis can also lead to predictions. A **prediction** is what you think will be the outcome of your experiment or data collection. Predictions are usually stated in an "if...then" format. For example, if meat is kept at room temperature, then it will spoil faster than meat kept in the refrigerator. More than one prediction can be made for a single hypothesis.

Here is a sample prediction for the acid rain hypothesis.

Prediction: If a plant is watered only with acid rain (which has a pH of 4), then the plant will grow at one-half its normal rate.

3. Test the Hypothesis After you have formed a hypothesis and made a prediction, it is time to test your hypothesis. There are different ways to test a hypothesis. Perhaps the most familiar way is by conducting a controlled experiment. A **controlled experiment** is an experiment that tests only one factor at a time. A controlled experiment has a **control group** and one or more experimental groups. All the factors for the control and **experimental groups** are the same except for one factor, which is called the **variable**. By changing only one factor (the variable), you can see the results of just that one change.

Sometimes, a controlled experiment is not possible due to the nature of the investigation. For example, stars are too far away, dinosaurs have been extinct for millions of years, and the Earth's core is surrounded by thousands of meters of rock. It would be difficult if not impossible to do controlled experiments on such things. Under these and many other circumstances, a hypothesis may be tested by making detailed observations. Taking measurements is one way of making observations.

4. Analyze the Results After you have completed your experiments, made your observations, and collected your data, you must analyze all the information you have gathered. Tables and graphs are often used in this step to organize the data.

5. Draw Conclusions Based on the analysis of your data, you should conclude whether your results support your hypothesis. If your hypothesis is supported, you (or others) might want to repeat the observations or experiments to verify your results. If your hypothesis is not supported by the data, you may have to check your procedure for errors. You may even have to reject your hypothesis and make a new one. If you cannot draw a conclusion from your results, you may have to try the investigation again or carry out further observations or experiments.

6. Communicate Results After any scientific investigation, you should report your results. By doing a written or oral report, you let others know what you have learned. They may want to repeat your investigation to see if they get the same results. Your report may even lead to another question, which in turn may lead to another investigation.

Say Cheese!

Purpose

Students study the effects of an acid on a protein solution. In the process, they will make two types of cheese.

Time Required

Two consecutive 45-minute class periods

Lab Ratings

EASY ———————→ HARD

TEACHER PREP

STUDENT SET-UP

CONCEPT LEVEL

CLEAN UP

Advance Preparation

This lab works well as an at-home lab or as an in-class lab for groups of 4–6 students. The activity requires the use of a sink, so if you choose to conduct it in class, make sure adequate sink space is available.

To simplify this activity, you may wish to skip the paneer-making portion of the lab. Otherwise, make sure the necessary equipment to drain the cheese and make paneer is available for overnight use. To drain the cheese, place it in cheesecloth and drain it overnight on a large screen over a sink or suspend it over a sink or bucket.

You may wish to have available crackers and fruit for students to enjoy with the cheese they make in this activity.

Safety Information

Instruct students to use caution when heating the milk. They should use insulated mitts when lifting the pan of hot milk. They should place the saucepan on a trivet or hot pad for cooling, turning the handle of the saucepan away from the edge of the table to avoid accidental bumping.

Teaching Strategies

Before beginning the activity, you may wish to define pH and review the range of values for pH with students. Point out that acids have a pH less than 7 and bases have a pH greater than 7, and that a pH of exactly 7 is neutral. Inform the class that the pH of distilled water is typically close to 7. You may wish to have the class verify this.

Background Information

You may also wish to explain why it is so important to maintain the correct pH in biological systems by sharing the following information: A protein is a chain of amino acids. Changing the pH of a protein solution can alter the solubility of the protein in the solution. It can also change the overall shape of the protein molecule. Both the solubility and the shape of a protein affect how the protein functions.

After completing the activity, you may wish to discuss other methods for changing the shape of a protein. These include changing the temperature and adding certain enzymes. The latter example is explored in "The Mystery of the Runny Gelatin" on page 11 of this booklet.

Evaluation Strategies

 For help evaluating this lab, see the Rubric for Performance Assessment in the *Assessment Checklists & Rubrics*.

This rubric is also available in the *One-Stop Planner CD-ROM*.

Peggy Belt
West Hardin Middle School
Cecillia, Kentucky

LIFE SCIENCE

LAB
1 **STUDENT WORKSHEET**

SKILL BUILDER

Say Cheese!

You may know that cheese is made from milk, but have you ever wondered exactly how cheese is made?

Well, milk contains a lot of protein and a lot of water. The protein is soluble—it is dissolved in the water. To make cheese, you first have to change the shape of the protein so that it is insoluble. When this happens, the protein clumps together to form a solid called *curd*. The leftover liquid part of the milk is called the *whey*.

So how do you change the shape of the protein? Easy! You change the acidity of the milk. In this lab, you will do just that. In the process, you will make two types of cheese: cottage cheese and *paneer,* a popular cheese in India.

MATERIALS

- pH paper and scale, pH range 1–8
- 250 mL of whole milk
- 8 mL of lemon juice
- hot plate
- saucepan
- 10 mL graduated cylinder
- stirring spoon
- hot pad or trivet
- potholder or oven mitt
- watch or clock that indicates seconds
- sieve or strainer
- 1.5 L bowl
- 3 pieces of cheese cloth, 30 × 30 cm
- twine or kite string, about 20 cm long
- sink or bucket
- water-filled pot or other heavy container
- knife
- paper plate

Objective

To make cheese by changing the acidity of a protein solution

On Your Whey!

Making curd is the first step in the making of any cheese. There is more than one way to make curd, but here you will do so by adding lemon juice to milk.

1. Using the pH paper, measure the pH of the milk and the lemon juice. Record your results in the table on page 3. You will fill in the final column later.

2. In the saucepan, heat the milk until it just begins to boil. **Caution:** Make sure the milk does not boil over the side of the saucepan.

3. Pour 8 mL of lemon juice into the milk. Stir the mixture once, and remove it from heat. Allow the mixture to cool for 15 minutes.

4. After 15 minutes, the milk should begin to curdle—the curd (solid) will separate from the whey (liquid). Measure the pH of the whey, and record your results in the table on page 3.

pH Test Results

	Milk	Lemon juice	Whey
pH			

5. Was the pH of the whey the same as that of plain milk? Why or why not?

_____

_____

_____

6. Line the sieve or strainer with three layers of cheesecloth, and place it in a sink. Pour the contents of the saucepan into the sieve or strainer.

7. Allow the curd to drain for 1 minute. You now have cottage cheese!

8. Do you think the whey contains the same amount of protein as plain milk contains? Why or why not?

_____

_____

_____

Near Paneer?

Now follow steps 9–12 to make *paneer*, a popular cheese in India.

9. Gather the edges of the cheesecloth and twist them over the sink, pressing out as much whey as possible.

10. Use the piece of twine to tie off the cheesecloth bag. Suspend the bag over a sink or bucket so that it will drain overnight.

11. In the morning, untie and loosen the bundle. Keeping the cheesecloth wrapped around the cheese, flatten the cheese slightly on top of the plate. Place the water-filled pot or other heavy object on top of the cheese for 4–5 hours.

12. At the end of this time, the cheese should be compressed to a thickness of 1.5–2 cm. Remove the weight and the cheesecloth. You now have paneer! The cheese is ready to be cut into cubes.

▲ LIFE SCIENCE

Are You a Cheese Whiz?

Critical Thinking

13. In this activity, you studied how changing the acidity of a protein's environment changed the solubility of the protein. This caused the protein to behave differently.

As another example of the importance of the environment on protein function, consider blood. Blood contains large quantities of dissolved proteins. Use your experience from this lab to predict what might happen to these proteins if blood pH suddenly dropped significantly.

_____

_____

_____

What might be a danger of such a drop in pH for circulatory function?

_____

_____

_____

Going Further

As milk curdles, the shape of the protein molecules in the milk changes, causing the protein to become insoluble. But what does it mean for a protein to change shape? Research the primary, secondary, tertiary, and quaternary structure of a protein molecule. Then write a short paragraph explaining what these structures are. Some changes to these structures will affect the function of the protein molecule.

DESIGN YOUR OWN

The Incredible Edible Cell

Cooperative Learning Activity

Group size: 3–4 students

Group goal: To apply a knowledge and understanding of cell organelles by developing an edible cell model

Positive interdependence: Each group member should choose a role, such as organelles coordinator, evaluation leader, cell designer, or materials coordinator.

Individual accountability: After the activity, each group member should be able to point out and explain the function of each organelle in the group's cell model.

Time Required

Two 45-minute class periods and a discussion period a few days before the activity begins

Lab Ratings

EASY ————————→ HARD

TEACHER PREP

STUDENT SET-UP

CONCEPT LEVEL

CLEAN UP

Advance Preparation

A few days before beginning the activity, divide the class into groups. Assign plant cells to half of the class and animal cells to the other half.

To prepare students for the model-building portion of this activity, review the various organelles in a cell and discuss whether each is found in a plant cell, an animal cell, or in both plant and animal cells. Also discuss how the shape and structure of each organelle is related to its function.

After the review, have students work in groups to brainstorm about food items they will use to represent each organelle. Encourage students to be creative in their choices of foods, but make sure the foods resemble the cell components that are being modeled. After the discussion, announce the day when students will build their model cells. Be sure to allow a few days for students to gather their assigned food items.

Each group will be responsible for bringing their chosen food items to class. Make sure that each student knows which food items they will be bringing for their group. You may wish for each group to submit a list of proposed foods to you for approval.

Before students begin constructing their models, give them a copy of the Peer Evaluation of Cell Model checklist on page 10 of this booklet so they know in advance how they will be graded. This checklist also provides a list of the basic parts of plant and animal cells, so students may find it helpful when creating their blueprints.

You may wish to prepare an example model cell for students to observe before they build their own models. Follow the instructions on a box of unflavored gelatin to make 1 L of gelatin liquid. Chill the gelatin in a mold for 1–2 hours before class (until it has partially set).

continued...

Tracy Jahn
Berkshire Junior High
Canaan, New York

Possible edible items for the organelles:

SAMPLE MATERIALS	
• green jelly beans	• raisins
• gummy worms	• licorice
• vitamin capsules, emptied	• round fruit (peach or plum)
• marshmallows	• fruit strips
• gumdrops	• grapes
• candied sprinkles	• lettuce

Helpful Hints

The shape of soft candies can be modified with scissors. Vitamin capsules will eventually dissolve in gelatin. By placing a capsule in the gelatin mold, you can create an empty space in the mold once the mold sets.

Safety Information

Make sure the students pour the hot water into their gelatin mold very carefully and slowly to avoid scalding. Students should clean their workspace and wash their hands upon completing the activity.

Teaching Strategies

Students may benefit from an explanation of why a three-dimensional model of a cell is useful. Explain that illustrations of a cell typically show only a cutaway view of the cell. The models they will build in this activity demonstrate that cell parts are spread throughout the volume of a cell just like a blueberry muffin has blueberries throughout its volume.

When the peer evaluations have been completed, you may wish to have students eat their cells!

Background Information

Robert Hooke, the first person to view microscopic cells, took the word *cell* from a word referring to the little rooms in a monastery. In fact, the Latin word *cell* means "little room." The boxes in a computer spreadsheet program are called cells because they function like little rooms in the program. Similarly, batteries contain one or more cells in which the chemical reactions that provide electrical energy occur.

Evaluation Strategies

The Peer Evaluation of Cell Model checklist on page 10 of this booklet is available to help evaluate student performance. After students have traded models, direct each group to fill out one of these checklists. When the evaluations have been completed, direct each member of the group to sign the bottom of the checklist and return it to the other group.

Each group should then review the evaluation of their model. Encourage discussion in and among the groups. When the discussion is complete, instruct each group to staple together the evaluation, the blueprint, and the sketch, and then hand the packet in to you.

 You may also wish to use the Teacher Evaluation of Cooperative Group Activity in the *Assessment Checklists & Rubrics*. This checklist is also available in the *One-Stop Planner CD-ROM*.

LAB 2 **STUDENT WORKSHEET**

DESIGN YOUR OWN

The Incredible Edible Cell

What do all these items have in common: spreadsheets, monasteries, batteries, armadillos, plants, and humans? Answer: they all contain cells. However, only armadillos, plants, and humans contain living cells. Inside all living cells are tiny structures called organelles—*little organs*—which help the cell function just like your organs help your body function.

Over the next few days, you will be part of a group that will create an edible model of a living cell. In doing so, you will gain a better understanding of the various parts of a cell that help it function.

LIFE SCIENCE

MATERIALS

- various food items of your choosing
- box of gelatin
- several rolls of plastic food wrap (for the cell membrane)
- transparent mold for gelatin, such as a heat-resistant bowl or baking dish
- 1 L of hot water
- stirring spoon
- refrigerator

Objective

To make an edible model of the cell

Getting Ready

1. Your teacher will assign your group a plant or animal cell to model. As a group, determine how you will go about creating your model by asking questions such as the following:

   - How do plant and animal cells differ?

   - What organelles are present in our cell?

   - What is the structure and function of each organelle in our cell?

   - What foods will we use to represent the organelles and other components of our cell?

   - Do our chosen foods accurately represent the structure of each organelle?

2. As a group, develop a blueprint of your cell model. Be sure to label each part of the cell and to write an explanation for your choices of foods. Be prepared to justify your choices for each organelle. Include a key at the bottom of your blueprint for reference.

3. Make a checklist of the food items and materials you will need in order to build your model cell. Each member of your group should be assigned one or more of these items to bring to class on the day of the activity.

4. Agree upon a place for gathering your food items and materials so that you have everything you need to make your edible cell.

The Incredible Edible Cell, continued

Day 1: Building a Larger-than-Life-Sized Model

5. Collect the materials your group has brought for your cell model, including all edible and non-edible items. Consult your checklist to make sure you have everything you will need. You are now ready to build!

6. The gelatin mold represents the cell wall (this may or may not be part of your model). Place a sheet of plastic wrap in the mold. This represents the cell membrane. Carefully pour the gelatin and hot water into the mold until the mold is about 75 percent full. The gelatin represents the cytoplasm, the liquid internal environment of a cell.

7. Add the foods you have chosen to represent the organelles into the gelatin, and stir the mixture.

8. Cover the completed mold with plastic wrap, and refrigerate it overnight so that your cell model will set.

Day 2: All Cells Are Not Alike

9. Remove your mold from the refrigerator, and study the structure of your model. As a group, make a key to identify the organelles in your model. A sample key is provided at left.

10. If you made an animal-cell model, trade your model with another group for a plant-cell model. If you made a plant-cell model, trade it for an animal-cell model.

11. Designate one member of the group to be the illustrator. With group input, the illustrator should draw a sketch of the other group's cell model. The illustrator should label the sketch, identifying all structures in the cell.

12. When you are finished, trade cells with the other group and compare your sketch with theirs.

13. Answer the questions on the next page individually.

Sample Animal Cell

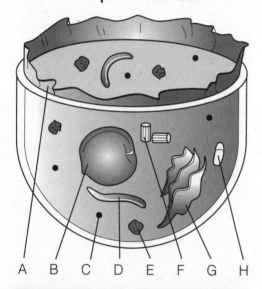

A B C D E F G H

KEY
A. cell membrane—plastic wrap
B. nucleus—plum
C. ribosome—candy sprinkles
D. endoplasmic reticulum—gummy worms
E. mitochondria—raisins
F. centriole—rope licorice
G. golgi complex—fruit strips
H. lysosome—empty vitamin capsule

The Incredible Edible Cell, continued

Analysis

14. How were the structures in the cell your group created similar to the structures in the cell you received from the other group?

_____

_____

_____

15. How did the cell structures differ?

_____

_____

_____

Critical Thinking

16. Explain any differences in the contents of a plant cell and an animal cell in terms of the function of the cell.

_____

_____

_____

_____

_____

_____

Going Further

Research a specialized cell, such as a nerve cell or a red blood cell. Then develop a blueprint for an edible model of that cell using edible items. In doing so, consider how the structures in the specialized cell differ from the structures in a typical animal or plant cell.

LIFE SCIENCE

Name _____ Date _____ Class _____

Student Evaluator _____

Peer Evaluation of Cell Model

SCORE

TYPE OF CELL   **PLANT   ANIMAL**   (circle one)

BASIC ELEMENTS _____ 1. Completed a cell blueprint

_____ 2. Completed a key for the model cell

_____ 3. Completed a written explanation of why particular foods were chosen to represent the organelles

_____ 4. Completed a written explanation of the function of each organelle

_____ 5. Completed a cell model

ACCURACY _____ 6. Included all the basic parts of the cell: (Circle missing items. Cross out items that should not have been in the cell)

- cell wall
- cell membrane
- nucleus
- ribosomes
- endoplasmic reticulum
- mitochondria

- centrioles
- chloroplasts
- golgi complex
- lysosome
- vacuole

_____ 7. Chose foods that represent the structure of different organelles

_____ 8. Represents the cell in three dimensions

_____ 9. Displays creativity

EFFORT _____ 10. Shows substantial effort

TOTAL POINTS _____ **OUT OF 30 POSSIBLE POINTS**

COMMENTS _____
(continue on back if
necessary) _____

_____

_____

_____

_____

_____

_____

SIGNATURES _____

DISCOVERY LAB

The Mystery of the Runny Gelatin

Cooperative Learning Activity

Group size: 3–4 students

Group goal: To study the ability of certain enzymes to break down a protein by adding several fresh fruits to gelatin

Positive interdependence: Each group member should choose a role such as a materials coordinator, data inputter, or assistant researcher.

Individual accountability: After the activity, each group member should be able to explain one effect of a protein-splitting enzyme on a certain protein's function.

LIFE SCIENCE ▲ ▲ ▲

Time Required

Two 45-minute class periods, or approximately 90 minutes at home over 2 days

Lab Ratings

EASY ————————————→ HARD

TEACHER PREP 🧪🧪🧪

STUDENT SET-UP 🧪🧪

CONCEPT LEVEL 🧪🧪🧪

CLEAN UP 🧪🧪

Advance Preparation

This activity requires a refrigerator. If one is not available in the classroom, you can assign this as an at-home activity.

If you choose to perform this activity in class, you will need to purchase samples of seven fresh fruits for this lab, or have students bring samples to class. Include at least one fruit that inhibits the gelling process, such as pineapple, fig, papaya, mango, or kiwi. Other fruits, including apples, bananas, oranges, grapes, tangerines, coconuts, strawberries, and peaches, do not affect the gelling process. Store the fruits in a cool place until you begin the activity.

You will also need to prepare the enzymes in a solution ahead of time. Do so by mixing 25 g of meat tenderizer with 250 mL of tap water. In order for the enzyme solution to work properly, the meat tenderizer should contain proteolytic

enzymes or *papain*. Papain is a protein-splitting enzyme derived from papaya. Most common meat tenderizers contain this enzyme, but check the ingredients to be sure.

Next prepare a large bowl of flavored or unflavored gelatin solution according to the directions on the box. Provide 100 mL samples of the gelatin solution for each group. This can be done by distributing the gelatin in small measuring cups or by placing the bowl of gelatin solution in a central location and having students use a ladle to fill their 100 mL beakers.

Be sure to provide a container of soapy water for the used stirring rods.

Finally, you will need to make enough 5 g (about 1 cubic cm) fruit samples so that each lab group has seven samples, one for each fruit. To ensure freshness, cut up the fruit on a cutting board just before beginning the activity. Thoroughly mash each fruit and place 5 g samples of each fruit in small (15 mL) paper cups. Be sure to use a clean instrument for mashing each new fruit sample to avoid contaminating the samples. Wooden craft sticks make good mashing instruments. You may choose to have students help you with this task on the first day of the activity.

continued...

Kevin A. Tierney
Rolling Hills Middle School
El Dorado, California

Safety Information

Before beginning this activity, ask students if they are allergic to any of the foods used in this lab. Students should avoid contact with any such foods. Instruct students to notify you as soon as possible if they have an allergic reaction.

Avoid prolonged contact with the enzyme solution, as papain can irritate the skin and mucous membranes. *Bromelain,* the protein-splitting enzyme found in pineapple, may irritate the mouth and tongue if it is eaten. Students should thoroughly wash their hands upon completing the lab.

Teaching Strategies

On the first day of the activity, review the function of enzymes with the class.

Emphasize that enzymes are proteins that help a chemical reaction to occur but do not themselves change or chemically react with the other substances in the reaction. You may also wish to discuss the mechanisms by which enzymes are inactivated, including an increase in heat or acidity.

Evaluation Strategies

For help evaluating this lab, see the Teacher Evaluation of Cooperative Group Activity in the *Assessment Checklists & Rubrics.* This checklist is also available in the *One-Stop Planner CD-ROM.*

DISCOVERY LAB

The Mystery of the Runny Gelatin

Chef Uva Plantana is famous for her magnificent molded fruit salads. A recent tour of the South Pacific inspired Uva to create a spectacular salad of fresh pineapples, papayas, apples, figs, oranges, kiwis, and bananas as an edible centerpiece for the Culinary Convention banquet. She was testing her concoction a day before when, to her horror, the gelatin failed to set. Her mold was a runny mess!

Uva called her friend Detective Hugo Naranja and said, "This has never happened before! You must help me find out what is wrong with my recipe."

"I'll be right there—don't touch a thing," Hugo responded. An hour later, Hugo entered the kitchen. "A juicy problem. . .," said Hugo. "Have you changed anything?"

"I prepared the gelatin just as I always have," Uva said shrugging, "but I usually use a mix of canned and fresh fruit. This time all the fruit was marvelously fresh." Uva narrowed her eyes. "What's gone wrong?"

"We should know in a few hours," said Hugo, rolling up his sleeves and grabbing a bowl. "Have an assistant bring me one of each type of fruit in the salad, some meat tenderizer, and a bowl of liquid gelatin."

Now you are the assistant. Follow Hugo's directions to help solve the mystery of the runny gelatin.

LIFE SCIENCE

MATERIALS

- marker
- 2 small (15 mL) empty paper cups
- 7 small (15 mL) paper cups with samples of 7 different fruits
- 5 mL of enzyme solution
- 100 mL of gelatin solution
- 2 paper plates
- sheet of plastic
- refrigerator
- small bowl or dish

Objective

To demonstrate the action of various fruit enzymes on a protein solution (gelatin)

Day 1: Hugo's Directions

1. Carefully read my note pad on page 14.

2. Use a marker to label the empty paper cups 1 and 2 and the seven filled paper cups 3 through 9.

3. Record the name of each fruit in the Gel Set Data Table on page 16.

4. Pour 5 mL of the enzyme solution into cup 2 only.

5. Add 10 mL of the gelatin solution to all nine cups.

6. Place the filled cups on paper plates, and cover them with plastic film. Place the cups overnight in the refrigerator.

7. What do you predict will happen to each of the samples? Record whether you think each sample will set by listing *yes* or *no* in the Gel Set Data Table on page 16.

Day 2: The Plot Thickens

8. On the next day, remove the tray from the refrigerator. Place a bowl or dish under each sample. Gently tip each cup to see whether the contents are soft and runny or are gelled and firm. If the mixture has gelled, write *yes* in the Gel Set column of the Data Table. If some of the contents begins to drip, write *no* in the Gel Set column.

9. Clean up as directed by your teacher.

10. Review the evidence and clues you've gathered in the Data Table and from Hugo's note pad. Then help Detective Naranja answer Ms. Plantana's questions.

NOTE PAD: *From the desk of*

H. Naranja

Important clues:

Enzyme—a protein that speeds up certain chemical reactions. Enzymes have a variety of functions, including breaking down other proteins

Bromelain—a protein-splitting enzyme in some fruit

Gelatin—a protein that forms a soft gel when mixed with warm liquid and that forms a firm gel when the liquid is cooled. Damaging this protein will prevent gel formation

Papain—a protein-splitting enzyme found in fruit; a common ingredient of some meat tenderizers

Hugo's Advice

11. Did the gelatin fail to set in any of the cups? If so, list the contents of those cups.

_____

_____

_____

_____

The Mystery of the Runny Gelatin, continued

12. What might the meat tenderizer have in common with the fruit(s) that kept the gelatin from setting?

_____

_____

_____

_____

_____

13. How did Uva's preparation differ this time from previous times?

_____

_____

_____

14. Based on what you have learned in this activity, what do you think happens to fresh fruit in the canning process? How would this affect the enzymes in the fruit?

_____

_____

_____

_____

Critical Thinking

15. Use what you have learned from this activity to help Uva revise her recipe.

_____

_____

_____

_____

The Mystery of the Runny Gelatin, continued

Gel Set Data Table

Sample	Contents	Prediction: Will the gel set?	Actual: Did the gel set?
1	liquid gelatin		
2	liquid gelatin with meat tenderizer		
3			
4			
5			
6			
7			
8			
9			

Going Further

Some people take tablets that contain enzymes from papaya and pineapple to counter the effects of indigestion. How do these tablets work?

Bacterial Buddies

Purpose

Students observe how certain bacteria cultures affect the acidity and preservation of milk.

Time Required

Two consecutive 45-minute class periods

Lab Ratings

EASY ———————→ HARD

TEACHER PREP — 3 flasks
STUDENT SET-UP — 2 flasks
CONCEPT LEVEL — 2 flasks
CLEAN UP — 2 flasks

Advance Preparation

A few days in advance, ask a few students to bring in saucepans and stirring spoons to use in making the yogurt. You will need one saucepan and one spoon for each group of 3–4 students. Be sure to label the utensils so they can be returned to the appropriate student after completing the activity.

This lab requires 12–16 beakers that must be kept overnight for each class. Therefore, you may wish to do this lab with only one or two classes at a time. The beakers should be thoroughly cleaned and dried before use to avoid contamination. If you want students to be able to eat the yogurt, you may wish to substitute jars for the beakers and substitute a measuring cup for the graduated cylinder.

You will also need to provide a baking dish in which students can place their beakers overnight. The dish should be filled halfway with warm (44°C) water. Identify a safe location in the classroom to place the dish overnight.

This lab also requires heated milk. You will have to allow some time for the milk to cool to about 44°C. Time-saving tip: Preheat the milk, and allow it to cool to the proper temperature before class begins.

The yogurt that students will prepare in this activity is edible, but you may still wish to provide students with a large sample of yogurt to eat when they have completed the lab. Bring in some honey or vanilla for students to flavor the yogurt, and some spoons and small cups.

Safety Information

Tell students to exercise caution when using the hot plate. They should be especially careful that no water spills out of the baking dish. Any water on an electrical appliance can lead to serious injury. Make sure all cords are secured to the floor and tabletops to help prevent accidents.

Be sure students clean their workspace after setting up the experiment.

Teaching Strategies

Remind students to use a fresh pH strip for each test. It takes approximately four hours for yogurt curds to form. The pH of the cultured milk will lower by approximately two points due to the bacterial production of lactic acid. The pH of the uncultured milk should change very little.

You might wish to have students check on their beakers after school. They should keep the beakers sealed and gently shake the beakers to check the consistency of the mixture.

Because the appearance and smell of uncultured milk that has sat overnight can vary, be prepared for a range of responses when students are describing the milk.

Evaluation Strategies

For help evaluating this lab, see the Rubric for Performance Assessment in the *Assessment Checklists & Rubrics*. This rubric is also available in the *One-Stop Planner CD-ROM*.

Bill Beeman
St. Paul Alternative
Learning Center
St. Paul, Minnesota

LIFE SCIENCE

LAB
4 **STUDENT WORKSHEET**

SKILL BUILDER

Bacterial Buddies

Many people think of bacteria as nasty and life-threatening, even though not all bacteria are harmful. In fact, some bacteria actually help us. Believe it or not, people add bacteria to food to help preserve it!

Milk will spoil quickly if it is not refrigerated. Ancient cultures found a way to preserve milk without refrigeration. They used certain types of bacteria to ferment the milk and turn it into yogurt. These bacteria feed on sugar in the milk, producing lactic acid in the process. The acid helps to prevent the growth of other, harmful bacteria and gives yogurt its sour taste.

In this lab, you will observe the fermentation of milk and the resulting change in acidity as milk turns into yogurt.

MATERIALS

- 300 mL of nonfat milk
- large saucepan
- cooking thermometer
- watch or clock
- oven mitts
- hot plate
- pH paper and color scale
- 100 mL graduated cylinder
- 200 mL beakers (2), one labeled "No culture" and the other "Culture"
- waterproof marker for labeling
- live yogurt culture
- stirring spoon
- dish towel

SCIENTIFIC **METHOD**

Ask a Question

1. How do some bacteria help to preserve milk by turning it into yogurt?

Conduct an Experiment

2. While wearing the oven mitts, heat the milk in the saucepan to a temperature of 80°C. Do not allow the milk to boil. Maintain the milk at 80°C for 5 minutes while stirring continuously. Remove the saucepan from heat. **Caution:** Be careful when working around the hot stove.

3. Let the milk cool to about 44°C.

4. Use the pH paper to measure the acidity of the milk in the saucepan.
   Starting pH of milk in the saucepan _____

5. Pour 150 mL of the warm milk into the beaker labeled "No culture."

6. Measure the pH of the live-culture yogurt.
   pH of premade, live-culture yogurt _____

7. Stir 20 mL of yogurt into the milk that remains in the saucepan, (150 mL) and mix well. Measure the pH.
   Starting pH of milk and yogurt mixture _____

Bacterial Buddies, continued

8. Pour the mixture into the beaker labeled "Culture."

9. Place both beakers in a place designated by your teacher, and then cover them with a dish towel.

10. After 24 hours, retrieve the beakers and evaluate the contents of each for pH, smell, and appearance. Record the results in the Yogurt Log on this page.

Yogurt Log

Beaker	Appearance	Smell	pH
No culture			
Culture			

Analyze the Results

11. How did the contents of the beakers differ in smell and appearance on the second day?

_____

_____

_____

_____

_____

_____

_____

▲ LIFE SCIENCE

12. Why was it important to have a beaker in which no live culture was introduced?

_____

_____

_____

_____

13. Which beaker showed the greatest change in pH? Why do you think that happened?

_____

_____

_____

_____

Draw Conclusions

14. Based on the results of this activity, how do you think the addition of live-culture yogurt helps to keep milk from spoiling?

_____

_____

_____

_____

Going Further

Are there other kinds of friendly bacteria besides those in yogurt? What are they, and how do they help living organisms?

Knot Your Average Yeast Lab

Purpose
Students demonstrate how the production of carbon dioxide causes yeast dough to rise. In the process, they make edible pretzels.

Time Required
Two 45-minute class periods

Lab Ratings
EASY ——————→ HARD

TEACHER PREP
STUDENT SET-UP
CONCEPT LEVEL
CLEAN UP

Advance Preparation
This activity requires a microwave oven. However, you may wish to see if there is a conventional oven available for use. If the pretzels are cooked in a conventional oven, they should be placed on a cookie sheet and cooked at 220°C (425°F) for 12–15 minutes. Students will need a large, flat surface for rolling and twisting their dough. The surface will also need to be kept floured so the dough does not stick to the surface. The recipe is for 10 pretzels. You will need to make enough dough so that all students have the opportunity to make a pretzel. If any uncooked dough remains, you may wish to have students take some home to be baked.

You may wish to perform the steps in Day 1 as a class demonstration. This will reduce the cost and the amount of materials needed.

Safety Information
Before students begin the activity, be sure they thoroughly clean and disinfect their food-preparation area. The pretzels will be extremely hot when they come out of the oven. Make sure students allow time for the pretzels to cool before handling. Students will be working with flour. To control the mess you may wish to tape a dropcloth to the floor.

Teaching Strategies
This lab is a useful review of the chemical reactions that occur when yeast are active. Active yeast convert sugar to carbon dioxide, water, alcohol, and usable energy through the process of fermentation. The alcohol evaporates during the baking process, but carbon dioxide bubbles are trapped in the dough. Heat kills the yeast, stopping the production of carbon dioxide. The dough continues to rise because the gas trapped in the dough expands.

Some students will choose the wrong beaker for the pretzel dough so that they can see what the pretzels will be like without yeast. If students choose the wrong beaker, make sure there are enough edible pretzels available from the other groups to go around. You may also wish to provide salt and mustard for the students to flavor the pretzels.

When cooking the pretzels in a microwave oven, you may want to experiment with the settings. If you cook several pretzels at once, you will need to increase the cooking time. Do not increase the power setting; the dough will quickly become too hard to eat. Pretzels cooked in a microwave do not brown as they do in a conventional oven.

Evaluation Strategies
For help evaluating this lab, see the Rubric for Performance Assessment in the *Assessment Checklists & Rubrics*. This rubric is also available in the *One-Stop Planner* CD-ROM.

Carol Lang
University School (ETSU)
Johnson City, Tennessee

LIFE SCIENCE

LAB
5 **STUDENT WORKSHEET**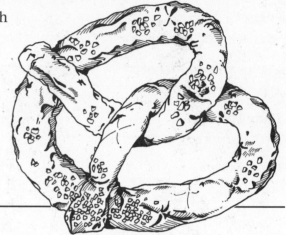

Knot Your Average Yeast Lab

Have you ever wondered what makes dough rise? Believe it or not, dough rises because of a fungus—a tiny, living, one-celled organism called *yeast*. When dried, yeast are in a state of suspended animation. But when you add warm water and sugar, watch out! The yeast get active and go into a feeding frenzy. What's left behind is carbon dioxide and alcohol.

In this activity, you can watch yeast at work!

MATERIALS

- 500 mL beakers (4) or jars
- waterproof marker for labeling
- 2 packages of active dry yeast
- 750 mL of warm water about 40°C
- 750 mL of hot water, approx 80°C
- 16 mL (3 tsp) of sugar
- thermometer
- 4 stirring spoons
- watch or clock
- mixing bowl
- 650 mL of all-purpose flour
- 8 mL (1½ tsp) of salt
- mixing spoon
- roll of plastic wrap
- refrigerator
- paper plates
- microwave
- paper towels

Objective

To observe the effects of yeast activity on pretzel dough

Day 1: Activate Those Yeast Cells!

1. Label the beakers 1–4. Add one-half package of yeast to each beaker.

2. Add ingredients to each beaker according to the following directions:

   Beaker 1: 325 mL warm water
   Beaker 2: 325 mL warm water and 8 mL sugar
   Beaker 3: 325 mL hot water
   Beaker 4: 325 mL hot water and 8 mL sugar

3. Using a separate stirring rod each time, gently stir the contents of each beaker. Wait three minutes.

4. Observe the contents of each beaker for a few seconds. What is happening in the beakers? Record and explain your observations in the chart on page 23.

5. What do your lab results tell you about the effect temperature has on the carbon-dioxide production of yeast?

   _____

   _____

   _____

   _____

   _____

Beaker Observations

Beaker 1: warm water and yeast	Beaker 2: warm water, yeast, and sugar
Beaker 3: hot water and yeast	**Beaker 4: hot water, yeast, and sugar**

6. Is sugar necessary for the yeast to produce carbon dioxide? Explain.

_____

_____

_____

_____

7. Select the beaker that is best-suited for making pretzels. Explain your choice.

_____

_____

_____

_____

LIFE SCIENCE

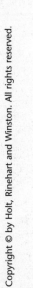

8. Pour the contents of the beaker you select into the mixing bowl. Make sure that all of the mixture is transferred to the bowl.

9. Add 125 mL of flour and 8 mL of salt to the yeast mixture, and mix well. Slowly add more flour until dough begins to form. You will add approximately 500 mL of flour. The remaining flour will be used to flour the kneading surface.

10. Sprinkle a handful of flour evenly on a large, flat surface. Turn the dough onto the floured surface, and begin to knead it. Knead by repeatedly pushing the palms of your hands into the dough. Every few seconds, turn the dough a quarter turn, and fold the dough over. You will need to add more flour to the surface of the dough and the table as the dough gets sticky. Continue kneading for about five minutes. Stop kneading when the dough no longer feels sticky and is smooth and elastic.

11. Place the dough back in the bowl. Cover the bowl with plastic wrap, and label it for your group. Refrigerate the dough overnight.

Day 2: Let's All Do the Twist!

12. Remove the dough from the refrigerator. What differences do you notice in the dough's appearance? Record your observations.

_____

_____

_____

_____

13. Using your observations from the day before, explain why the dough's appearance has changed.

_____

_____

_____

_____

_____

14. Pull off a piece of dough the size of a golf ball, and roll it into a long, snakelike shape. Fold the dough into a pretzel shape using the diagrams below as your guide.

  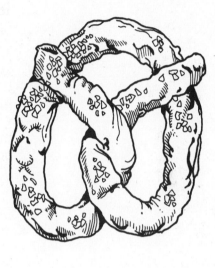

HELPFUL HINT

The pretzels will not turn brown in a microwave oven—do not overbake them.

15. Place the unbaked pretzels on paper plates. Cook them in the microwave at low to medium (30%) power for 2–3 minutes. Your pretzels are ready when they are dry and slightly springy to the touch.

16. Carefully remove the pretzels from the oven, and allow them to cool for five minutes.

17. Break a piece off the end of the pretzel, and look inside.

What Happened?

18. What does the inside of the pretzel look like?

_____

_____

_____

19. What caused the inside of the pretzel to look like it does?

_____

_____

_____

▶ LIFE SCIENCE

20. Do you notice any evidence of the alcohol that the yeast produced? Explain your answer.

_____

_____

_____

_____

_____

_____

21. If you had used the contents of a different beaker to make the dough, how might the pretzels have been different?

_____

_____

_____

_____

_____

Critical Thinking

22. The heat from the oven killed the yeast and no more carbon dioxide was produced. So why did the dough continue to rise during the baking process?

_____

_____

_____

_____

_____

Not Just Another Nut

Purpose

Students dissect a peanut seed and peanut sprout to observe, identify, and compare embryonic plant structures and functions.

Time Required

Two 45-minute class periods approximately one week apart

Lab Ratings

EASY ——————————→ HARD

TEACHER PREP

STUDENT SET-UP

CONCEPT LEVEL

CLEAN UP

ADDITIONAL MATERIALS

To grow sprouts for each student pair:
- small, clear plastic cup
- 100 mL of fine-grained vermiculite
- 2 peanut seeds with reddish brown seed coats intact
- water
- growth lamp or direct sunlight (per class)

Advance Preparation

Plant the peanut seeds one week before the dissection so that students will have a good-sized sprout to observe. You might want to assign this task to students so they can care for their sprouts and observe their growth. Peanut plants normally grow outdoors. If you choose to grow your plants indoors, make sure they have plenty of direct sunlight, or place them under growth lamps.

Growing sprouts: For each plant, fill a small, clear plastic cup with perlite. Dig a small hole a few centimeters deep, and place two peanut seeds in the hole. Cover the peanut seeds with perlite, and pat the perlite lightly. Putting more than one peanut seed in each cup increases the probability that a sprout will grow in each cup. Check the cup daily to ensure that the perlite remains moist.

Preparing seeds for dissection: The day before performing the activity, place raw, unshelled peanuts in warm water, and soak overnight.

Safety Information

Although the peanuts and peanut sprouts that students handle in this activity are edible, instruct students not to eat the peanuts or sprouts for sanitary reasons. You may wish to provide additional peanuts for students to eat after they have finished the dissection.

Teaching Strategies

This activity works best when performed in pairs. You may wish to have students compare the peanut-seed structure with the structure of lima beans or peas.

Evaluation Strategies

Student drawings should clearly identify the structure of the peanut during each stage of development. All structures should be clearly labeled.

For help evaluating this lab, see the Rubric for Performance Assessment in the *Assessment Checklists & Rubrics*.

This rubric is also available in the *One-Stop Planner CD-ROM*.

LIFE SCIENCE

Carol Lang
University School (ETSU)
Johnson City, Tennessee

LAB
6   **STUDENT WORKSHEET**

DISCOVERY LAB

Not Just Another Nut

You might be surprised to hear that peanuts aren't nuts at all. Also known as goobers, groundnuts, or earthnuts, peanuts are legumes. Legumes are the fruit of a particular type of plant. Unlike most legumes, peanuts ripen underground instead of aboveground. In the southern United States, the tops of peanut plants are used to feed livestock.

In this activity, you will look at the peanut seed and peanut sprout in greater detail.

MATERIALS

- paper plate
- raw, unshelled peanut seed pod, soaked overnight
- toothpick
- magnifying glass
- cup containing peanut sprout

USEFUL TERMS

seed coat
reddish, paper-thin covering around each peanut seed

hilum
a scar on the seed indicating where the seed was attached to the fruit

cotyledons
nutrient-heavy, fleshy halves of the legume seed

embryonic leaves
tiny leaves inside the seed

embryonic root
rootlike part inside the seed

SCIENTIFIC
METHOD

Make a Prediction

1. What is the function of a peanut seed in the growth of a peanut plant?

_____

_____

_____

Make Observations

2. On the paper plate, carefully open the peanut seed pod to retrieve the seeds inside. Gently open one of the seeds by sliding the two halves past each other. Use the toothpick if needed.

3. Examine each half of the seed with the magnifying glass. Use the Useful Terms at left to identify as many structures as you can.

Collect Data

4. Sketch both halves of the peanut seed in the space provided on page 30. Label the following parts: embryonic leaves, embryonic root, cotyledons, hilum, and seed coat.

Not Just Another Nut, continued

Copyright © by Holt, Rinehart and Winston. All rights reserved.

USEFUL TERMS
primary root root of the sprout **shoot** stem and leaves of the sprout

5. Remove the peanut sprout from the cup, and carefully examine the plant. Sketch the sprout in the space provided on page 30. Use the Useful Terms to identify and label the parts.

Analyze the Results

6. Compare your sketches for the peanut seed and the sprouted peanut. What structures have changed as the plant has grown?

_____

_____

_____

_____

Draw Conclusions

7. What do you think is the purpose of the hard shell that you removed from the peanut at the beginning of the lab? (Hint: Think about where the fruit of the peanut plant grows.)

_____

_____

_____

8. How would you explain the change in the appearance of the cotyledons in the sprout?

_____

_____

_____

Going Further

George Washington Carver was a scientist who urged farmers in the southern United States to plant peanuts. He is known for researching and developing more than 300 products from peanuts. Find out why he encouraged farmers to grow peanuts, and list at least five products that he derived from peanuts.

LIFE SCIENCE

Legume Observations

Peanut (seed)

Peanut (sprout)

Here's Looking at You, Squid!

Cooperative Learning Activity

Group size: 2–3 students

Group goal: To dissect and identify the parts of a common ocean invertebrate in order to relate structure and function

Positive interdependence: Each group member should choose a role, such as dissection leader, discussion leader, or materials coordinator.

Individual accountability: After the activity, each group member should be able to identify the major parts of a squid and explain the function of each part.

Time Required

One 45-minute class period

Lab Ratings

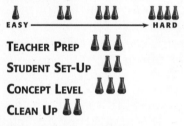

EASY ————————→ HARD

TEACHER PREP
STUDENT SET-UP
CONCEPT LEVEL
CLEAN UP

Advance Preparation

You will need one whole, edible squid per student group. Such squids are available frozen, in bulk, from large grocery stores.

A dissection knife works best in this activity. However, very sharp scissors will also work if a dissection knife is not available.

You may wish to have an electric frying pan, oil or butter, flour, and salt handy to fry the squid mantles and arms for the class to enjoy after completing the activity. Do so only if the squid has been left unrefrigerated for no more than one hour.

Students may be interested to know that squid is also known as *calamari*. To make fried calamari, mix the cut pieces of squid with the flour and salt. Let them sit on wax paper for 10 minutes before placing them in the heated oil or butter. When cooking is complete, drain the calamari on paper towels, and serve with lemon wedges or a red cocktail sauce. Be sure you do not overcook the squid; it can become tough and rubbery.

ADDITIONAL MATERIALS

- the mantle and tentacles from 1 squid
- small bag of flour
- pinch of salt
- electric frying pan
- oil or butter, enough to coat the pan
- lemon wedges
- red cocktail sauce
- paper plates
- paper towels
- forks
- spatula

Safety Information

Instruct students to be very careful when using sharp tools. Students should also thoroughly wash their hands after dissecting the squid.

Before beginning this activity, ask students if they are allergic to any of the foods used in this lab. Students should avoid contact with any such foods. Instruct students to notify you as soon as possible if they have an allergic reaction.

Teaching Strategies

Students are asked to consider the possible functions of various structures in the squid body. If they are having difficulty, you may wish to help them by offering suggestions for possible functions.

continued...

Georgiann Delgadillo
Continuous Curriculum School
Spokane, Washington

Review with students the diagram of squid anatomy on page 33. You may wish to have students sketch their squids on a separate piece of paper.

Language Arts Connection

To get students excited about the lab, you may wish to read to them an excerpt from Chapter 18 of Jules Verne's classic science-fiction novel, *20,000 Leagues Under The Sea*, in which there is a fictional encounter with a giant squid. You will find a brief excerpt describing the squid below. As you read the excerpt to the class, you may wish to explain any unfamiliar terms, such as *cephalopod*, *mollusc*, *poulp*, or *cuttlefish*.

"I looked in my turn, and could not repress a gesture of disgust. Before my eyes was a horrible monster worthy to figure in the legends of the marvellous. It was an immense cuttlefish, being eight yards long. It swam crossways in the direction of the Nautilus *with great speed, watching us with its enormous staring green eyes. Its eight arms, or rather feet, fixed to its head, that have given the name of cephalopod to these animals, were twice as long as its body, and were twisted like the furies' hair. One could see the 250 air-holes on the inner side of the tentacles. The monster's mouth, a horned beak like a parrot's, opened and shut vertically. Its tongue, a horned substance, furnished with several rows of pointed teeth, came*

out quivering from this veritable pair of shears. What a freak of nature, a bird's beak on a mollusc! Its spindle-like body formed a fleshy mass that might weigh 4,000 to 5,000 lb.; the varying colour changing with great rapidity, according to the irritation of the animal, passed successively from livid grey to reddish brown. What irritated this mollusc? No doubt the presence of the Nautilus, *more formidable than itself, and on which its suckers or its jaws had no hold. Yet, what monsters these poulps are! what vitality the Creator has given them! what vigour in their movements! and they possess three hearts! Chance had brought us in presence of this cuttlefish, and I did not wish to lose the opportunity of carefully studying this specimen of cephalopods. I overcame the horror that inspired me, and, taking a pencil, began to draw it."*

After students complete the dissection, you may wish to revisit this excerpt and ask the class how the squids they dissected differ from Verne's portrayal of a giant squid in this passage.

Evaluation Strategies

For help evaluating this lab, see the Observation of Cooperative Group in the *Assessment Checklists & Rubrics*.

This checklist is also available in the *One-Stop Planner CD-ROM*.

SKILL BUILDER

Here's Looking at You, Squid!

In Jules Verne's classic science-fiction novel, *20,000 Leagues Under the Sea*, the heroes battle a deadly giant squid that threatens to crush the hull of a submarine. Although giant squids do exist, most of us have only encountered their smaller, more timid relatives. Yet even the smaller squid looks like the stuff of science fiction. The top of the squid's head is actually a combined body-tail unit called a *mantle*. The head has two large eyes and is surrounded by two long tentacles and eight arms with rows of round suckers underneath. Underneath the head is a small opening to the funnel. The squid forces a jet of water through the funnel to propel itself backward or forward. Two fins are attached to the tail end of the squid to help it steer. Although the squid doesn't have a backbone, it does have a hard internal structure called a *pen*.

Now *you* can take a closer look at the unusual features of a squid.

LIFE SCIENCE ▲ ▲ ▲

MATERIALS

- squid
- paper plate
- magnifying glass
- dissection knife
- paper towels

Objective

To identify a number of structures and their functions in a squid, an aquatic invertebrate

Propel Yourself into Squid Dissection

1. Your teacher will provide you with a squid. Lay the squid flat on the plate, and examine it closely. Use the diagram below to help you identify the external parts of the squid.

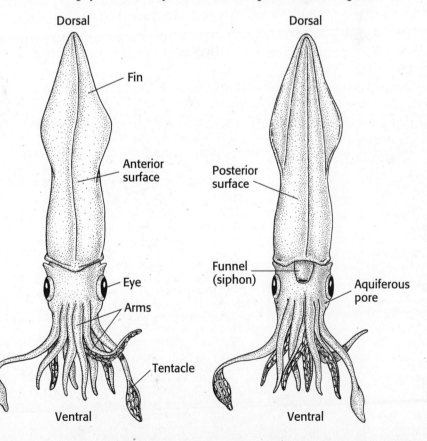

2. Use the magnifying glass to examine the suckers. How do you think the structure of the suckers helps the squid?

_____

_____

_____

3. The squid's arms and tentacles both have suckers, but the suckers serve different functions. Describe what functions you think the different suckers might serve.

_____

_____

_____

_____

_____

_____

4. Spread apart the arms, and look in the center of the squid. You will see a small black structure. Rub your finger over it, and describe what you observe.

_____

_____

_____

5. What do you think the function of this structure is?

_____

_____

_____

_____

6. Using the dissection knife, carefully remove the mantle from the head. Make a cut down the side of the mantle, and spread the mantle open on the plate. Use the diagram on page 35 to help you identify as many internal structures as you can.

Here's Looking at You, Squid! continued

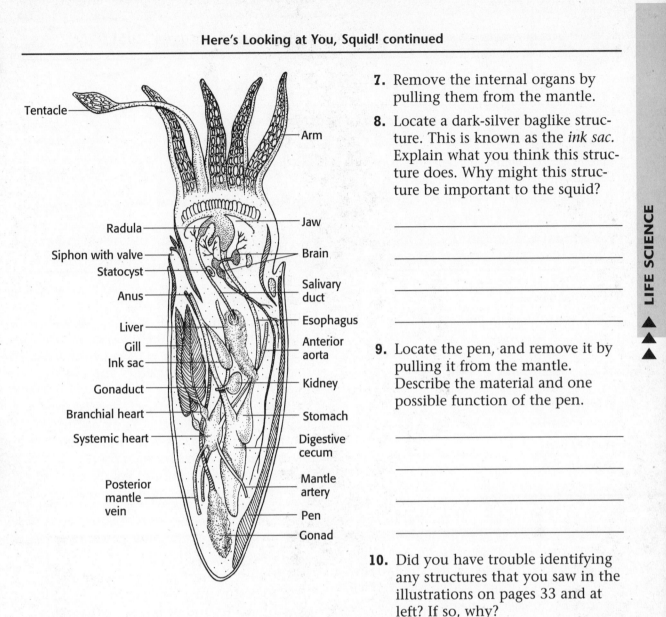

Tentacle

Arm

Radula

Jaw

Siphon with valve

Brain

Statocyst

Anus

Salivary duct

Liver

Esophagus

Gill

Anterior aorta

Ink sac

Gonaduct

Kidney

Branchial heart

Stomach

Systemic heart

Digestive cecum

Posterior mantle vein

Mantle artery

Pen

Gonad

7. Remove the internal organs by pulling them from the mantle.

8. Locate a dark-silver baglike structure. This is known as the *ink sac*. Explain what you think this structure does. Why might this structure be important to the squid?

_____

_____

_____

_____

9. Locate the pen, and remove it by pulling it from the mantle. Describe the material and one possible function of the pen.

_____

_____

_____

_____

10. Did you have trouble identifying any structures that you saw in the illustrations on pages 33 and at left? If so, why?

_____

_____

_____

11. Explain two ways squid and human anatomies are similar and two ways they are different.

_____

_____

_____

_____

DISCOVERY LAB

Why Birds of a Beak Eat Together

Cooperative Learning Activity

Group size: 4–6 students

Group goal: To use models of various bird beaks to study how adaptations help birds survive in a particular habitat

Positive interdependence: Each group member should choose a role, such as timer, recorder, feeder, and presenter.

Individual accountability: After the activity, each group member should be able to explain which habitat their beak was best suited for and why.

Time Required

One 45-minute class period

Lab Ratings

EASY ————————→ HARD

TEACHER PREP

STUDENT SET-UP

CONCEPT LEVEL

CLEAN UP

Advance Preparation

Set up six stations around the room. Each station will serve as one of the habitats described in the chart on page 37. At each table, provide the listed materials and display a card describing the habitat. You will also need to provide six kitchen implements to model six beak adaptations, as follows. Label each utensil with the name of the corresponding bird.

Bird Information

Model beak	Bird
1. spoon with slots or holes	duck
2. large tongs	heron
3. short straw or an eyedropper	hummingbird
4. small tweezers	warbler
5. fork	hawk
6. pliers	finch

Safety Information

Caution students not to eat any food at any of the stations. Students should also exercise caution when working with sharp objects, such as the tweezers, fork, or pliers.

Before beginning this activity, ask students if they are allergic to any of the foods used in this lab. Students should avoid contact with any such foods. Instruct students to notify you as soon as possible if they have an allergic reaction.

Teaching Strategies

This activity is designed to accommodate a total of six groups. If a large class size dictates that you must have groups of more than four students, you can include additional habitats and beaks. For example, a small plastic cup could be used to represent the beak of a whippoorwill, which eats flying insects. The insects could be represented by popcorn thrown into the air.

continued...

Elizabeth Rustad
Crane Junior High
Yuma, Arizona

Before beginning the activity, you may wish to discuss with your students the concepts of natural selection and adaptation. Natural selection is the process by which organisms that are best suited to their environment survive and reproduce. Adaptation is a change in an organism's structure that helps it live and reproduce successfully in its environment.

Assign each flock to an initial station. Tell the flocks that they will be given two minutes at each station to obtain as much food as they can from the station. They should start only on your signal.

You may wish to have extra food samples available for the students to enjoy after completing the activity.

Evaluation Strategies

Request that students hand in their feeding charts upon completion of the activity. This chart will provide an indication of the critical thinking each student applied in this activity.

For help evaluating this lab, see the Group Evaluation of Cooperative Group Activity in the *Assessment Checklists & Rubrics*. This checklist is also available in the *One-Stop Planner CD-ROM*.

LIFE SCIENCE

Station Information

Station	Materials	Habitat description
1	Cereal flakes in a large bowl of milk (water may be substituted for milk)	Small plants floating in a lake
2	Bran flakes and raisins moistened with milk (or water) in a large bowl	Small animals buried in mud
3	Jar filled halfway with juice or powdered drink mix; cap on jar removed	A flower filled with nectar
4	Jelly beans buried in crumpled aluminum foil	Small insects living in tree bark
5	Cubes of cheese or bread	Small rodents
6	Peanuts covered with cereal flakes in a shallow bowl	Leaves and nuts buried on the forest floor

Name _____ Date _____ Class _____

DISCOVERY
LAB

Why Birds of a Beak Eat Together

You are part of a group of hungry birds looking for a good place to eat. How do you know how to find such a place? Well, it depends on the type of food available in the area and how easily you can get to the food.

Luckily, there are many types of feeding habitats nearby. In this activity, you and your flock will fly to each one of the habitats and try to obtain food.

Happy flying and good eating!

MATERIALS

- One of the following tools: spoon with slots or holes, large tongs, short straw or eye-dropper, small tweezers, fork, or pliers
- plastic cup

Objective

To model the beak adaptations of birds and study how effective the adaptations are in obtaining various types of food

Let's Get Pecking, Birds!

1. Your teacher will provide your flock with a model of a beak and a plastic cup. Six different feeding "habitats" are arranged around the room. Your flock's job is to determine the habitat your beak is best suited for. First walk around the room and examine each habitat. Then predict in which habitat you think it will be easiest to obtain food. Record your prediction below.

_____

_____

_____

SAFETY ALERT!

Exercise caution when working with sharp objects such as tweezers, forks, or pliers.

WARNING

Do not eat the food you collect!

2. Move to your first habitat, and designate one student to obtain the food.

3. When your teacher signals to begin, have this student use the "beak" to collect as much food as possible in the time allotted. The collected food should be transferred to the plastic cup.

4. When your teacher signals to stop, discuss with your flock how easy it was to get food in this habitat. Record your results in the Feeding Chart on page 39.

5. Return the collected food to the station, leaving the station for the next group in the same condition as you found it.

6. Move around the room to each habitat. At each habitat, repeat steps 3–4. Be sure that every student contributes to the discussions.

Feeding Chart

Habitat	Feeding results
1	
2	
3	
4	
5	
6	
7	

Beak-ause All Birds Are Different

7. In which habitat was it easiest for your flock to obtain food? Explain.

_____

_____

_____

LIFE SCIENCE

8. How does your answer compare with your prediction at the beginning of this activity?

_____

_____

_____

_____

_____

9. Based on the results of this activity, why do you think beaks have adapted the way they have?

_____

_____

_____

Critical Thinking

10. What would happen if the habitat to which your flock were best suited were destroyed? Are there any other habitats in which your flock could easily survive? Justify your answer.

_____

_____

_____

_____

Going Further

Watch a video about the eating habits of birds that live in different habitats. Then discuss with the rest of the class what you learned from the video.

DISCOVERY LAB

LIFE SCIENCE

A Salty Sweet Experiment

Purpose

Students determine the areas of the tongue that are most sensitive to sour, sweet, bitter, and salty tastes.

Time Required

One 45-minute class period

Lab Ratings

EASY ———————→ HARD

TEACHER PREP
STUDENT SET-UP
CONCEPT LEVEL
CLEAN UP

Advance Preparation

Obtain toothpicks for students to use as sample applicators. Also have on hand distilled water, which will be used to cleanse the palate between tastings. Prepare taste samples for the following four categories:

• **Sour**—fresh lemon juice

• **Sweet**—15 mL granulated sugar per 250 mL distilled water

• **Bitter**—freshly brewed strong coffee

• **Salty**—15 mL table salt per 250 mL distilled water

For each group, pour 5 mL of each of the taste samples in small plastic cups, and label the cups "sour," "sweet," "bitter," and "salty." Distribute the cups, and toothpicks before you begin the activity. Keep the box of toothpicks in a central location in case students need extras.

Safety Information

Students should not use each other's toothpicks. Be sure that only the approved taste samples are used. Provide alternative food samples for students who are allergic to one or more of the suggested food items. For example, vinegar may be substituted for lemon juice and cream of tartar mixed in a little distilled water can replace coffee.

Teaching Strategies

This activity is best performed in pairs. Have each student taste the samples in a different order and record their answers on their own copy of the data table.

Evaluation Strategies

For help evaluating this lab, see the Rubric for Performance Assessment in the *Assessment Checklists & Rubrics*. This rubric is also available in the *One-Stop Planner CD-ROM*.

Patricia Marks
San Marcos Middle School
San Marcos, California

LAB

9 **STUDENT WORKSHEET**

DISCOVERY LAB

A Salty Sweet Experiment

Tondy Presser dropped her cup of hot chocolate. "I burned the tip of my tongue!" she exclaimed.

"Hold on," you say as you hand her your bowl and a spoon. "Eat some of my ice cream to cool the burn." Tondy quickly takes a few bites of the ice cream and makes a face. "Yuck! It's salty."

You give her a puzzled look. "That's odd. The ice cream tastes very sweet to me. Do you think the burn on your tongue is affecting your sense of taste?"

MATERIALS
• 4 taste samples in small cups, 5 mL each
• cup of water
• bandanna
• 10 toothpicks

SCIENTIFIC METHOD

Ask a Question

Which areas of the tongue are most sensitive to sour, sweet, bitter, and salty tastes?

Make Observations

1. Your teacher will provide you with four cups containing the taste samples and one cup containing water. Before beginning the experiment, make sure your partner has no allergies to any of the taste samples. If necessary, ask your teacher for substitutes to the samples you have.

2. Decide which student in your pair will be blindfolded first. This student should cover his or her eyes with the bandanna. The other student should performs steps 3–6 below.

3. Examine the diagram on this page, and locate region A on your partner's tongue. Dip the end of a toothpick into the first taste sample. Lightly touch a spot in that area with the toothpick.

4. Have your partner identify the taste (sour, sweet, bitter, or salty) and the strength of the taste (strong, weak, or no taste). Record the results in the Taste Response table on page 43. Discard the toothpick, and have your partner take a sip of water to wash the taste sample from his or her mouth.

5. Repeat steps 3–4 for the remaining taste samples in region A. Be sure that you use a new toothpick for each taste sample and that your partner rinses with water between each sample. Record your partner's responses in the table.

6. Repeat steps 3–5 for regions B, C, and D of the tongue. Enter the response to each substance in your table.

7. Now switch roles with your partner, and repeat steps 1–6.

8. When both partners have finished sampling the tastes on all four areas of the tongue, compare your results, and answer the following questions.

Taste Response

Region of the tongue	Sample type	Strength of taste (first taster)	Strength of taste (second taster)
A	Sour		
	Sweet		
	Salty		
	Bitter		
B	Sour		
	Sweet		
	Salty		
	Bitter		
C	Sour		
	Sweet		
	Salty		
	Bitter		
D	Sour		
	Sweet		
	Salty		
	Bitter		

LIFE SCIENCE

A Salty Sweet Experiment, continued

Analyze the Results

9. According to your results, which areas of the tongue were most sensitive to the following tastes?

Sour: _____

Sweet: _____

Bitter: _____

Salty: _____

10. Which regions of the tongue, if any, detected only one taste sensation?

_____

_____

_____

Draw Conclusions

11. Tondy was unable to taste the sweetness of the ice cream. Give one explanation for this.

_____

_____

_____

_____

_____

_____

12. Why might the ice cream have tasted salty to Tondy?

_____

_____

_____

_____

_____

_____

A Salty Sweet Experiment, continued

13. Most deadly poisons are extremely bitter. What would be the advantage of having the back part of the tongue detect only bitter tastes?

_____

_____

_____

_____

_____

_____

_____

_____

▶ **LIFE SCIENCE**

Going Further

Foods do not always taste the same to different people. Amaranth, a grain, is one such food. Research amaranth to learn more about what it tastes like to different people and what causes this variation.

Snack Attack

Purpose

Students test a variety of snack foods for their relative fat content.

Time Required

One and a half 45-minute class periods

Lab Ratings

EASY ——————————→ HARD

TEACHER PREP
STUDENT SET-UP
CONCEPT LEVEL
CLEAN UP

Advance Preparation

Gather six low-fat and regular samples of various snack food items, such as cheese, potato chips, candy bars, and cookies. Finely crush each of the items. Place 2 g of each sample in a small cup for each group. Peel and finely chop samples of avocado and apple, and then mash the samples or use a food processor if one is available. Place 2 g of each of these samples in a small cup for each group.

Bring the packages from the various snack items to class so students can read the nutritional labels. Or you may wish to bring a photocopy of each label for each group.

You may wish to put the food samples for the class in a central location to make it easier for students to collect their samples.

Safety Information

Students should be careful when using the scissors.

Teaching Strategies

The serving size for each item will vary. Because the actual fat content varies depending on the serving size, it is easier for students to compare percentages of fat for portions of the same weight.

When performing the experiment, it may be easier for students to see the size of the fat stain by holding the test panel up to the light. The stained paper will be translucent, and the students will be able to mark where the light passes through. When trying to determine why the stains may have shrunk, students might think that the fat evaporated. You may need to encourage them to correctly relate the shrinking stains to water evaporation.

The fat content for an avocado is 16 percent, while an apple has no appreciable fat content. Because the diameter of the fat stain directly relates to the percentage of fat in the food samples, students should be able to calculate the fat content for the avocado and the apple.

Evaluation Strategies

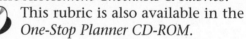 For help evaluating this lab, see the Rubric for Performance Assessment in the *Assessment Checklists & Rubrics*. This rubric is also available in the *One-Stop Planner CD-ROM*.

Randy Christian
Stovall Junior High
Houston, Texas

SKILL BUILDER

Snack Attack

Elizabeth Goose is throwing the party of the year, but health-conscious Jack Spratt eats only foods that are low in fat. Liz gave him a list of foods she is planning to serve at the party, but Jack is worried—he doesn't know how to tell the fatty foods from the low-fat foods. Can you help him figure out what foods he should eat at the party?

MATERIALS

- large brown paper bag
- scissors
- metric ruler
- 6 samples of various snack foods
- avocado
- apple
- nutritional labels from the various snack foods used
- paper towels

Objective

To determine the relative amount of fat in a variety of snack foods

Day 1: Getting Ready

1. Cut the front and rear panels from a paper bag.

2. Draw a grid with 3 columns and 3 rows on the panel of brown paper. Each square in the grid should be about 10×10 cm.

3. You will be testing eight food samples. Place one sample in the center of a square on the grid. Label the square for that sample.

4. Repeat step 3 for each of the other samples.

5. Label the test panel with your group information, and set it in a place where it will be undisturbed for 24 hours.

Day 2: Finding That Sneaky Fat

6. Retrieve your test panel, and carefully remove and discard the food from the paper.

7. Observe any differences in the paper in each square. Can you tell where the fat was absorbed by the paper? Explain.

_____

_____

_____

_____

_____

_____

LIFE SCIENCE

8. Measure the diameter of the circles that remain on the paper. In ascending order of size, record the substances and measurements in the Fat-Content Results Table below.

Fat-Content Results Table

Food sample	Diameter of fat stain (cm)	Percentage of fat

9. Read the nutritional label for each packaged snack and record the percentages of total fat for each snack on the chart. What is the relationship between the diameter of the fat stain and the percentage of fat for the packaged foods?

_____

_____

_____

10. Compare the size of the fat stains for the avocado and the apple with the size of the fat stains for the other foods. Use those comparisons to estimate the percentage of fat for the avocado and the apple. Record your answers in the chart.

What Should Jack Eat?

11. Which food left the stain with the largest diameter?

_____

_____

12. Which food contained the highest percentage of fat?

_____

_____

_____

13. Which two foods should Jack eat to avoid fat?

_____

_____

_____

14. Which two foods should Jack avoid? Explain your answer.

_____

_____

_____

Critical Thinking

15. You may have noticed when testing the apple sample that a large circle appeared and then disappeared. What do you think happened?

_____

_____

Going Further

Some fats are healthier than others. Fats may be monounsaturated, polyunsaturated, or saturated. Avocados are very high in monounsaturated fat. Find out why the type of fat you eat may be just as important as the amount of fat you eat.

▲ LIFE SCIENCE

Famous Rock Groups

Purpose

Students model various aspects of the rock cycle, including mechanical weathering, sedimentation, metamorphism, and igneous rock formation.

Time Required

One 45-minute class period

Lab Ratings

EASY ———————————→ HARD

TEACHER PREP

STUDENT SET-UP

CONCEPT LEVEL

CLEAN UP

Advance Preparation

Purchase four types of different-colored candy baking chips, such as peanut butter, dark chocolate, white chocolate, and butterscotch. Portions of chips may be premeasured with a 50 mL beaker and placed in disposable cups to facilitate distribution to students. Different-colored baking bars and a cheese grater may be substituted to aid in making shavings.

Safety Information

Remind students to exercise extreme caution when using sharp instruments, such as scissors or knives. When using the hot plate, students should wear oven mitts and exercise caution.

Teaching Strategies

This activity works best in groups of 3–4 students. You may wish to review the rock cycle with students before beginning the activity. Emphasize the basic types of rock (igneous, sedimentary, metamorphic), and review the processes by which they are formed.

Explain to students that this lab emphasizes one path through the rock cycle. Remind students that there are many paths through the rock cycle. In fact, any type of rock can become any other type of rock. To make sure there is no confusion on this point, you may wish to review the diagram below.

Similarly, in this lab the force of gravity is the only factor mentioned in the conversion of sedimentary rock into metamorphic rock. Remind students that other factors can play a role in the creation of metamorphic rock, such as tectonic activity, chemical changes, and cementation.

Evaluation Strategies

For help evaluating this lab, see the Rubric for Performance Assessment in the *Assessment Checklists & Rubrics*.

This rubric is also available in the *One-Stop Planner CD-ROM*.

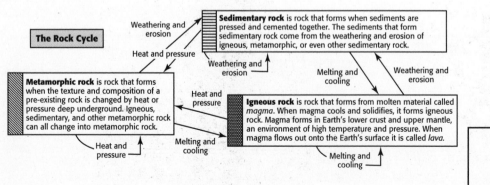

The Rock Cycle

Sedimentary rock is rock that forms when sediments are pressed and cemented together. The sediments that form sedimentary rock come from the weathering and erosion of igneous, metamorphic, or even other sedimentary rock.

Metamorphic rock is rock that forms when the texture and composition of a pre-existing rock is changed by heat or pressure deep underground. Igneous, sedimentary, and other metamorphic rock can all change into metamorphic rock.

Igneous rock is rock that forms from molten material called *magma*. When magma cools and solidifies, it forms igneous rock. Magma forms in Earth's lower crust and upper mantle, an environment of high temperature and pressure. When magma flows out onto the Earth's surface it is called *lava*.

Weathering and erosion
Heat and pressure
Weathering and erosion
Melting and cooling
Weathering and erosion
Heat and pressure
Heat and pressure
Melting and cooling
Melting and cooling

Elizabeth Rustad
Crane Junior High
Yuma, Arizona

**LAB
11 STUDENT WORKSHEET**

**MAKING
MODELS**

Famous Rock Groups

When is a rock a liquid? When it melts, of course! But melting is just one part of the rock cycle.

A rock can follow many paths in the rock cycle. For example, a molten rock cools and hardens to form igneous rock. Mechanical weathering or erosion can later break the rock down into tiny particles. These particles build up in layers to form sedimentary rock. As the layers accumulate, their weight adds pressure to lower layers, and the combined heat and pressure can compress the rock below to create metamorphic rock. When the temperature and pressure become great enough, the metamorphic rock melts. The cycle can then continue on the same pathway or a completely different pathway.

In this activity, you will get a chance to make a tasty model of one pathway through the rock cycle.

MATERIALS

- sheet of waxed paper
- 4 types of candy chips, 50 mL each
- 4 sharp knives or scissors
- heavy aluminum foil, 25 × 25 cm
- metric ruler
- 2 large, heavy books (such as dictionaries or large textbooks)
- aluminum pie plate, 20 cm in diameter or larger
- hot plate
- 2 oven mitts

Objective

To simulate the formation of sedimentary, metamorphic, and igneous rock

A Chip Off the Old Rock

1. Cover your work area with a sheet of wax paper, and place one of the types of chips on it. Shave the chips into small pieces with a knife or scissors. **Caution:** Be careful not to cut yourself!

2. Repeat step 1 for the other chips, making sure to keep the shavings in separate piles.

3. In your model of the rock cycle, what do the following items represent?

   • The whole chips: _____

   _____

   • The knife or scissors: _____

   _____

   • The chip shavings: _____

   _____

4. Fold the sheet of aluminum foil in half. Place the foil on your workspace, and open it so that the crease is in the middle.

EARTH SCIENCE

USEFUL TERMS

mechanical weathering
processes that change the physical form of rocks, such as erosion

sedimentary rock
rock formed from other rocks as a result of intense heat, pressure, or chemical processes

metamorphic rock
rock formed from other rocks as a result of intense heat, pressure, or chemical processes

igneous rock
rock formed from cooled and hardened magma (molten rock)

5. Sprinkle one type of chip shavings to one side of the crease in the foil within a 4 × 4 cm square. Pat the shavings to make an even layer, and use the edge of the knife to scrape the shavings into the square. Be careful not to tear or cut the foil.

6. Repeat step 4 with the other three types of shavings, making layers of each flavor on top of the previous layer of shavings. Each layer represents a layer of sediment.

7. Fold the top half of the foil over the chip layers. Place this foil package between two heavy books, and apply light pressure for 2 seconds. Remove the foil package from the books, and open the package.

8. What has occurred?

_____

_____

9. What kind of rock formation did this simulate?

_____

_____

_____

_____

10. What do the books represent in this simulation?

_____

_____

_____

_____

_____

_____

11. Place the candy-chip "rock" back in the foil, and put the foil between the two books again. This time, two students should press as hard as possible against the books for one minute. Remove the package from between the books, and open the package.

Famous Rock Groups, continued

Name ___ Date ___ Class ___

12. What happened to the layers of chips this time?

13. What rock process does this simulate?

14. What does pushing the books down represent in this simulation?

SAFETY ALERT!
- Place the oven mitts on now.
- Do not touch the hot foil package! Be careful working with the hot plate.

15. Now place the aluminum pie plate on the hot plate. Then place the package in the pie plate, and turn on the hot plate. Be sure the package is open slightly at the top so that you can observe what happens.

16. What is happening to the chips?

17. What does the hot plate represent?

EARTH SCIENCE

Copyright © by Holt, Rinehart and Winston. All rights reserved.

LABS YOU CAN EAT **53**

18. Turn off the hot plate, and allow your rock model to cool and harden completely. What type of rock does the cooled candy simulate? Explain your answer.

_____

_____

_____

_____

_____

19. Explain two ways the simulation in this lab does not accurately portray the rock cycle that occurs in nature.

_____

_____

_____

_____

_____

_____

_____

Going Further

Visit a local area of geologic interest, such as a road cut on a highway, and identify as many different types of rocks as you can. Make a rough sketch of the rocks and the rock formations, and discuss how they might have been formed.

GeoPancakes

Purpose

Students construct a model showing sedimentary rock layers, two types of unconformities, and two types of igneous rock intrusions.

Time Required

One 45-minute class period

Lab Ratings

EASY ——→ HARD

TEACHER PREP
STUDENT SET-UP
CONCEPT LEVEL
CLEAN UP

Advance Preparation

Choose a pancake mix that requires only the addition of water to prepare. Adjust the proportions of mix and water as necessary to make pancakes 1 cm thick. You may wish to premeasure the pancake mix for each group.

A large, flat-surfaced, electric griddle set on medium heat works best. You will need two to four griddles in class, assuming four pancakes are cooked at one time. You may wish to prepare the pancakes in advance, but fresh pancakes may be easier to work with.

Green or blue food coloring is likely to be most effective in this activity.

Safety Information

All students working with the griddle should wear oven mitts. Tell students to exercise extreme caution while working near the griddles. Make sure all cords are secured to the floor and tabletops to help prevent accidents. Students should also be careful when using a knife.

Teaching Strategies

This lab works best when students work in pairs. Before beginning this activity, students may benefit from a review of how sedimentary rock, unconformities, dikes, and sills are formed.

After completing the activity, you may wish to allow students to eat their geopancake models, or provide additional pancakes for students to enjoy.

As an extension, students could construct new rock profiles that differ from the one formed in this activity. Student groups could then trade rock profiles and analyze the history of the other group's geopancake layers.

Evaluation Strategies

The student sketch of the geopancake profile is useful in evaluating student performance. Make sure that these drawings clearly identify all changes to the rock layers and show each layer in its proper position in the profile.

For help evaluating this lab, see the Rubric for Performance Assessment in the *Assessment Checklists & Rubrics*.

This rubric is also available in the *One-Stop Planner CD-ROM*.

EARTH SCIENCE

CLASSROOM TESTED & APPROVED

Kenneth Creese
White Mountain Junior High
Rock Springs, Wyoming

LAB
12 | **STUDENT WORKSHEET**

MAKING MODELS

GeoPancakes

Scientists often analyze the layers of rock in the Earth's crust to learn about the Earth's history. When sedimentary rock forms as thin layers are sandwiched together, the layers can be compared to the pages in a book. Over time, many layers in the Earth's "history book" are moved, torn, pulled out, or turned upside down.

In this lab, you will use colored pancakes to represent different sedimentary rock layers. You will then alter your model to represent various changes in the geologic record.

MATERIALS

- 250 mL of pancake mix
- 200 mL of water
- mixing bowl
- mixing spoon
- 30 mL of vegetable oil
- pancake griddle
- oven mitt
- metric ruler
- spatula
- paper plate
- bottle of food coloring
- mug or small bowl with a 10 cm diameter
- bread knife
- fork
- tube of chocolate frosting
- plastic drinking straw
- tube of vanilla cake frosting

Objective

To model geologic processes that affect the formation of sedimentary rock layers

Let's Get Cooking!

1. Pour the pancake mix and the water into a mixing bowl. Mix until smooth.

2. Spread a small amount of oil over the griddle's surface. When the griddle is warm, pour enough batter onto the griddle to make a pancake about 1 cm thick and 10 cm in diameter. **Caution:** Exercise caution and wear the oven mitts when you are near the hot griddle.

3. Cook the pancake until its bottom side is golden brown. Then flip the pancake and cook the other side. When the pancake is golden brown on both sides, remove it and place it on the paper plate to cool.

4. Before cooking the next pancake, you will need to add food coloring to the remaining batter. This will ensure that each pancake will be darker than the one cooked before it. Follow the instructions below to determine the correct amount of food coloring to add to each pancake.

- To make the **second** pancake, add **1** more drop of food coloring to the batter. Stir until the batter is evenly colored.

- To make the **third** pancake, add **3** more drops of food coloring to the batter. Stir until the batter is evenly colored.

- To make the **fourth** pancake, add **6** more drops of food coloring to the batter. Stir until the batter is evenly colored.

- To make the **fifth** pancake, add **9** more drops of food coloring to the batter. Stir until the batter is evenly colored.

HELPFUL HINT

A mug or small bowl with a 10 cm diameter makes a great "cookie cutter" to ensure that your cooked pancakes are all the same size.

5. When you have colored the batter for a pancake, reapply oil and cook the pancake as described in step 3. Then repeat the process until all the pancakes have been cooked, stacking the pancakes in the order in which they were cooked. Allow the pancakes to cool for a few minutes before continuing.

6. Inspect the stack from the side. You have now made a model of a sedimentary rock profile!

Next let's see how changes in the layers affect the appearance of your model.

Formations in the Flapjacks

7. Using the spatula, gently lift the top four pancakes in the stack while a partner removes the bottom pancake. Your partner should then cut the bottom pancake into 10 strips one centimeter wide. Place the strips on their sides, cut side down, next to one another on the plate. The strips of the bottom pancake should now be vertical. Carefully lower the stack of pancakes onto the pancake strips. What kind of geologic formation is represented by this change?

_____

_____

_____

_____

8. Explain how this kind of geologic formation might occur in a real rock layer.

_____

_____

_____

_____

_____

EARTH SCIENCE

GeoPancakes, continued

9. Remove the fourth pancake (second from the top) from the stack, and tear it in half. Discard one half. Take the remaining half, and scrape it with the fork until it is very thin and has a number of holes in it (the less left of the pancake, the better). Replace the thin pancake half in its original place in the stack.

   What kind of geologic formation have you just modeled? Explain.

   _____

   _____

   _____

   _____

   _____

10. Place the chocolate-frosting nozzle between the second and third pancakes. Insert a stream of frosting, moving the nozzle back and forth so that the second pancake is completely covered with frosting.

    What kind of geologic formation did you model this time? Explain.

    _____

    _____

    _____

11. Make a hole in the stack of pancakes by puncturing all but the top pancake layer with a straw. Do not punch through the top pancake. Remove the straw. Place the vanilla-frosting nozzle into the hole, and insert a stream of frosting.

    What kind of geologic formation does this represent? Explain.

    _____

    _____

    _____

GeoPancakes, continued

SAFETY ALERT!
Be careful when using a knife.

12. While holding the stack of pancakes together, slowly cut the pancake stack in half with a bread knife. In doing so, make sure that you will be able to view all of the formations you have created. Carefully separate the two halves of the stack.

13. Observe the pancake profile you have created. Sketch the profile in the space provided here, and label the geologic layers and features you have represented.

EARTH SCIENCE

GeoPancakes, continued

Critical Thinking: Summing Up
Your GeoPancake's History

14. A geologist friend of yours sees your geopancake model and exclaims, "Wow! That looks just like a rock profile I saw in the field the other day! Can you tell me how the rock profile formed?" Use your experience of building a geopancake model to write a short narrative describing the history of the rock profile. Be sure to start with the oldest features and to mention as many geologic processes and features as possible, such as deposition, unconformities, erosion, and intrusions.

_____

_____

_____

_____

_____

_____

_____

_____

_____

_____

_____

_____

_____

Going Further

A third type of unconformity is a *nonconformity*. Suggest a method of using geopancakes to model this type of unconformity.

MAKING MODELS

Rescue Near the Center of the Earth

Purpose

Students create three-dimensional edible models of the interior structure of the Earth, including the inner core, the outer core, the mantle, and the crust.

Time Required

One 45-minute class period

Lab Ratings

EASY → HARD

TEACHER PREP 🧪🧪🧪
STUDENT SET-UP 🧪🧪
CONCEPT LEVEL 🧪🧪
CLEAN UP 🧪🧪🧪

Advance Preparation

Noninstant powdered milk works better than instant powdered milk. If neither is available, confectioner's sugar may be substituted, but extra sugar will be needed. Earth's outer core is a liquid, so strawberry and grape jelly work well because they are slightly runny. Marmalades, preserves, and jams will not work as well because they are too thick. When complete, the Earth balls will be approximately 4–5 cm in diameter.

Crush the graham crackers before class. You may also wish to make a sample of the peanut butter, powdered milk, and honey mixture before class to determine how much honey is needed to make a stiff, claylike dough. The amount of honey will vary with the consistency of the peanut butter. Be sure students have access to drinking water because this lab is likely to make them thirsty.

Safety Information

Make sure students thoroughly wash their hands before and after the activity. Students should be careful when using sharp objects.

Teaching Strategies

This activity works best in groups of 4–6 students. Before beginning, review the interior structure of the Earth using a diagram or three-dimensional model. You may also wish to discuss ways in which the model fails to accurately represent the Earth. For example, the extreme temperatures and pressures in the Earth cannot be easily depicted in a model.

The story in the activity is based on the information in the Earth Travel Data Chart below, which gives the thickness of each layer of the Earth and the mission's travel time through each layer of the Earth. The travel time through each layer is based on a speed of 12.5 km/h. You may wish to point out that oil drills usually go only 900–5,000 m into the Earth's crust and never into the Earth's mantle.

Evaluation Strategies

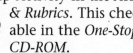 For help evaluating this lab, see the Teacher Evaluation of Cooperative Group Activity in the *Assessment Checklists & Rubrics*. This checklist is also available in the *One-Stop Planner CD-ROM*.

Earth Travel Data Chart

Layer of Earth	Thickness of layer (km)	Travel time
Crust	30	about 2.5 hours
Mantle	2,900	9.7 days
Outer Core	2,250	7.5 days
Inner Core	1,200	4 days

Georgiann Delgadillo
Continuous Curriculum School
Spokane, Washington

▶ **EARTH SCIENCE**

Name _____ Date _____ Class _____

Rescue Near the Center of the Earth

Mission Control has lost contact with its expedition! Dr. Julie Verne and her students are on a mission to explore the center of the Earth. Their last progress report was due on Day 17, and it is now 2 days overdue. You fear the team is in trouble. You must plan a rescue mission, but first you need to pinpoint the team's last reported location. The following are the progress reports you've received:

Day 1: Today we began our adventure by drilling with rock hammers at a constant rate of 12.5 km/h. Weather conditions were perfect at a mild and sunny 20°C. By late morning, we switched to the steam shovels to dig into less rocky, softer material. The team was forced to put on cooling suits as the heat became unbearable. The last recorded temperature today was 1,400°C. All is well.

Day 5: We're still digging with the steam shovels, but it's getting hotter. Today the temperature of the surrounding rock reached 3,000°C. The material is similar to clay, and as we pushed through we saw the rocks slowly flow back and obscure our trail.

Day 9: Wow! It is getting very hot down here. The temperature is 3,500°C. We're still using the steam shovels, but we're very glad our special cooling suits are working. The pressure-resistant coils in the suits are working overtime.

Day 10: Yesterday we stopped using the steam shovels and climbed into our mini-submarine. The heat is incredible—almost 6,000°C. Everything around us is liquid, but in our super heat-resistant, specially pressurized submarine we are going full speed ahead.

Your mission: build a model of the Earth. Then look for clues in the model and use the progress reports to find team members and bring them back safely.

MATERIALS

- set of metric measuring cups
- 125 mL of creamy peanut butter
- 65 mL of powdered milk
- bowl
- mixing spoon
- 65 mL of honey
- metal spoon
- sheet of wax paper
- plastic knife
- 125 mL of jelly
- 4–6 chocolate chips
- 125 mL of graham cracker crumbs

HELPFUL HINT

Avoid handling the mixture too much, or it could soften into a gooey mess.

USEFUL TERMS

crust
the thin outermost layer of the Earth

mantle
the thick layer of rock between the Earth's crust and core

outer core
the layer immediately surrounding the inner core of the Earth

inner core
the center of the Earth

Ask a Question

What is the interior structure of the Earth like?

_____

_____

_____

Make a Model

1. Wash your hands thoroughly.

2. Put 125 mL of peanut butter and 65 mL of powdered milk in the bowl. Mix them with a spoon. Add about one third of the honey to the mixture. Keep adding honey or powdered milk a little at a time until the dough feels like stiff clay.

3. Gather a rounded spoonful of dough approximately 5 cm in diameter (about a thumb's length), and roll it into a ball.

4. Place the ball on a piece of waxed paper, and carefully cut the ball in half. Be careful not to squash the ball when you cut it.

5. Using the tip of the spoon or your finger, scoop out a small hole in the center of each half of the ball. The holes should be about the size of the tip of your index finger.

6. Spoon a small amount of jelly into the holes you have scooped out. Place a chocolate chip in the middle of the jelly in one of the halves of the ball.

7. Place the two halves of the ball together, and roll the ball on the wax paper to seal the seam.

8. Pour the graham-cracker crumbs on the piece of wax paper. Roll the ball in the crumbs to thoroughly coat it. You now have a model of the Earth!

9. Place your model Earth on a paper plate. Carefully cut the ball in half again to see the interior of your model Earth. Each of the layers in your model has a texture similar to the texture of the corresponding layer in the Earth.

Using the model you've created and Dr. Verne's progress reports, you are now ready to report to Mission Control.

Collect Data

Begin your rescue plan by organizing what you know.

10. Fill in the second column of the chart on page 64 with the name of the corresponding Earth layer.

11. Fill in the third column of the chart on page 64 using one piece of information from your model and one piece of information from the story.

▲ EARTH SCIENCE

Model Analysis Chart

Model layer	Earth layer	Description of Earth layer
Graham-cracker crumbs		
Peanut butter mixture		
Jelly		
Chocolate chip		

Analyze the Results

12. Which layer of the Earth did the team reach by the end of Day 1?

_____

_____

_____

13. Which part of your model represents this layer?

_____

_____

_____

14. On Day 10, the team members continued their journey in the mini-submarine. Describe the layer of the Earth they must have entered in the submarine. How is this layer represented in your model?

_____

_____

_____

Draw Conclusions

15. Where will you send the rescue team to look for Dr. Verne and her students? Explain your answer.

_____

_____

_____

_____

16. Assume the team is at the place of their last transmission. Was there a layer that the team did not reach? If so, how was it represented on the model? Explain your answer.

_____

_____

_____

_____

_____

_____

EARTH SCIENCE

Going Further

Did you know that the interiors of some other planets in our solar system have a layered structure similar to Earth's? Choose a planet, and find out about its interior structure. Then make a sketch of the planet's structure. Be sure to identify similarities and differences between the planet you chose and Earth.

MAKING MODELS

Cracks in the Hard-Boiled Earth

Purpose

Students model some basic interactions of crustal plates—divergent boundaries, convergent boundaries, and transform boundaries—using the relative movement of shell fragments on a hard-boiled egg.

Time Required

One 45-minute class period

Lab Ratings

EASY ——————————> HARD

TEACHER PREP
STUDENT SET-UP
CONCEPT LEVEL
CLEAN UP

Advance Preparation

Prepare one hard-boiled egg per student. Cover eggs with water in a large saucepan or stockpot, and bring the water to a boil on a range top or Bunsen burner. Adjust the burner so that the water does not boil too rapidly (violent boiling may crack eggshells), and continue to boil for 15 minutes. Drain the water carefully, and rinse the eggs in cold tap water. If the hard-boiled eggs are stored overnight, they should be refrigerated.

You may wish to provide additional hard-boiled eggs for students to enjoy when they have completed the lab. If so, also consider having available salt or various spices, such as paprika, for students to sprinkle on their eggs before eating them.

If food coloring and paintbrushes are not available, you can substitute water-based markers. However, please note the safety concern below.

Safety Information

You may wish to use water-based markers instead of paintbrushes and food coloring. If so, be sure that students do not eat the eggs they use for this activity.

Teaching Strategies

You may wish to review the differences among the three types of plate boundaries before beginning this activity. Step 4, on page 67, may require some practice. Make sure that students do not squeeze the egg so hard it is destroyed.

Evaluation Strategies

For help evaluating this lab, see the Rubric for Performance Assessment in the *Assessment Checklists & Rubrics*.

This rubric is also available in the *One-Stop Planner CD-ROM*.

CLASSROOM TESTED & APPROVED

Lee Yassinski
Sun Valley Middle School
Sun Valley, California

LAB 14 · STUDENT WORKSHEET

MAKING MODELS

Cracks in the Hard-Boiled Earth

The Earth's crust is made up of large plates that are in constant motion. As two adjacent plates move in two different directions, one of three types of *plate boundaries* is formed: *divergent, convergent,* or *transform* boundaries. Identifying these plate boundaries helps scientists better understand the processes occurring in the Earth. It can also serve a practical purpose, such as predicting earthquakes.

In this lab, you will use a hard-boiled egg to model the motion of crustal plates on the Earth's surface.

MATERIALS

- hard-boiled egg
- paper towels
- thin paintbrush
- small bottle of food coloring
- magnifying glass

USEFUL TERMS

convergent boundary
the boundary between two tectonic plates that push directly into one another

divergent boundary
the boundary between two tectonic plates that move away from one another

transform boundary
the boundary between two tectonic plates that slide past each other

 SCIENTIFIC METHOD

Ask a Question

What effects does the movement of crustal plates have on the Earth's surface?

Conduct an Experiment

1. Place the egg on the paper towel, and lightly tap the egg in different places to produce cracks of various lengths and sizes. Be careful not to tap too hard.

2. Dip the paintbrush in the food coloring, and trace a number of the large cracks to make them more visible.

3. Sketch both the front and rear views of the egg in the space provided on page 68, and show where the cracks are located. (See the illustration above.)

4. Gently squeeze the egg until slight movement occurs between the pieces of the shell. Use the magnifying glass to help you see the motion. You should be able to distinguish at least three types of motion between the pieces of the shell. Squeeze the egg in different ways to create these types of motion. Indicate on your sketch the motion of the eggshell pieces.

Analyze the Results

5. What do the egg and the pieces of shell represent?

_____

_____

_____

EARTH SCIENCE ▲ ▲ ▲

Cracks in the Hard-Boiled Earth, continued

Egg Sketches

Front view of egg	Rear view of egg

6. What do the cracks in the shell represent?

_____

_____

_____

7. Describe the patterns created by the cracks in the shell.

_____

_____

_____

_____

_____

_____

8. Describe the three types of motion and their effects on the pattern of cracks.

_____

_____

_____

_____

_____

9. Relate these three types of motions to the three types of plate boundaries mentioned on page 67.

_____

_____

_____

_____

Draw Conclusions

10. Look up the definitions for the following landforms:

- caldera
- volcano
- mountain range
- aquifer
- rift valley
- delta
- strike-slip fault
- cirque

Which of these landforms can be associated with the three types of plate boundaries? Identify the type(s) of motion.

_____

_____

_____

_____

_____

_____

_____

EARTH SCIENCE

11. What are two weaknesses of using a hard-boiled egg to model the motion of the Earth's crustal plates?

_____

_____

_____

_____

_____

_____

_____

_____

_____

_____

_____

_____

Going Further

You can also use a hard-boiled egg to model the interior structure of the Earth. Using a knife, slice the egg from this activity in two (including the shell), and identify which parts of the Earth the shell, the egg white, and the egg yolk represent. Note at least one strength and one weakness in this model.

Dough Fault of Your Own

Purpose

Students demonstrate how the processes of folding and faulting shape rock formations.

Time Required

About $1\frac{1}{2}$ hours at home or two 45-minute class periods

Lab Ratings

EASY ———————————→ HARD

TEACHER PREP
STUDENT SET-UP
CONCEPT LEVEL
CLEAN UP

Advance Preparation

This lab makes an excellent at-home activity. Before assigning the lab to students, you may wish to perform it yourself at home. You may also wish to demonstrate in class how to properly cut and stack the cookie-dough layers. Colored clay works well for this demonstration.

If this activity is done in two class periods, begin Day 2 with "Breaking Even," on page 73. A wooden dowel may be substituted for the rolling pin.

Safety Information

Instruct students to be careful when using knives.

Teaching Strategies

You may wish to discuss rock folding and faulting with students before assigning this at-home activity.

Background Information

Point out that folding generally occurs gradually and deep in the Earth, where the intense heat and pressure make the rocks plastic and pliable. Rocks closer to the Earth's surface form faults instead of folds because these rocks tend to be brittle and break more easily under stress.

Evaluation Strategies

For help evaluating this lab, see the Self Evaluation of Lesson in the *Assessment Checklists & Rubrics*. This checklist is also available in the *One-Stop Planner CD-ROM*.

EARTH SCIENCE

Lee Yassinski
Sun Valley Middle School
Sun Valley, California

Name _____ Date _____ Class _____

MAKING MODELS

Dough Fault of Your Own

Different types of rocks respond differently when under intense heat and pressure. Rocks heated deep in the Earth become plastic and bend to form *folds*, while those near the surface tend to break and slip against one another to form *faults*. In this lab you will use cookie dough to model different types of folds and faults. When you're finished, your lab material can be baked into cookies!

MATERIALS

- large mixing bowl
- 225 mL (1 cup) of margarine or butter, softened
- 450 mL (2 cups) of sugar
- electric mixer
- 15 mL (3 tsp) of baking powder
- 10 mL (2 tsp) of vanilla extract
- 3 mL ($\frac{1}{2}$ tsp) of salt
- 2 large eggs
- 675 mL (3 cups) of all-purpose flour
- heavy mixing spoon
- medium-sized mixing bowl
- 120 mL ($\frac{1}{2}$ cup) of unsweetened cocoa
- large mixing bowl
- 3 sheets of wax paper or coated freezer paper, 30 × 50 cm
- rolling pin
- metric ruler
- knife
- permanent marker
- freezer
- watch or clock

Optional

- cookie sheet
- oven
- oven mitts

Objective

To demonstrate how the processes of folding and faulting shape rock formations

Rolling in Dough

You will first make three models of a slab of rock. The rocks are made up of four rock layers whose color alternates between light and dark.

1. In the large bowl, beat the butter and the sugar together until they are blended. Continue to beat rapidly until the mixture is light and fluffy. Mix in the baking powder, vanilla extract, salt, egg, and 560 mL ($2\frac{1}{2}$ cups) of the flour. Blend well.

2. To create the dough for the light-colored layers in your models, place half of the dough in a medium bowl. Stir in the rest of the flour and mix well.

3. To create the dough for the dark-colored layers in your models, stir the cocoa into the dough in the large bowl. Mix well.

4. Use your hands to form the dark-colored dough into a ball.

5. Place the ball of dough on a piece of wax paper. Flatten the ball slightly with the base of your palm.

6. Grip both ends of the rolling pin. Place the pin in the center of the dough, and roll the pin steadily over the dough. Continue to roll the dough until you have an even layer that is about 1 cm thick.

7. Using the ruler and the knife, cut the rolled dough into six 5 × 10 cm strips. If there are not enough strips, gather the remaining dough scraps and reroll them. Discard excess dough.

8. Clean and dry the rolling pin. Repeat steps 4–7 for the light-colored dough.

Copyright © by Holt, Rinehart and Winston. All rights reserved.

Dough Fault of Your Own, continued

USEFUL TERMS

shortening
the process of moving two spots on the Earth's crust closer together

folding
bending of rock layers made flexible by heat and pressure during shortening

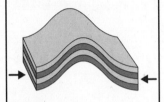

fault
a break between pieces of rock that move relative to one another

transverse or strike-slip fault
a nearly vertical fault in which rock moves both horizontal and parallel to the fault line

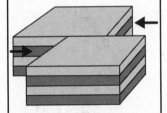

reverse fault
an angled fault in which one side of rock is pushed above the other during shortening

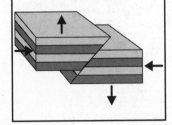

9. Stack a light strip on top of a dark strip. Add another dark strip, then add another light strip. You should now have a stack alternating dark and light layers of dough. Set this stack aside.

10. Repeat step 9 twice to make two more stacks.

11. Wrap one stack in a piece of waxed paper, and label it "Stack A." Place Stack A in the freezer for at least 20 minutes.

12. Place another stack on its side so that the alternating colors face upward. Cut the stack in two pieces at a 45° angle to the layers. Wrap each piece in a separate piece of wax paper. Label both pieces "Stack B," and place them in the freezer for at least 20 minutes.

Dough Shortening

13. Place the third stack on a desk or table that touches a wall with one of the short ends flush against the wall. With the base of your palm, compress the dough by pushing the opposite end of the stack toward the wall. What happens to the layers of dough?

_____

_____

_____

14. What geologic process is represented in this model?

_____

_____

_____

15. Where would such a process occur? Explain your answer.

_____

_____

_____

Breaking Even?

16. Remove Stack A from the freezer, and unwrap it.

17. Without allowing the dough to warm, crack the dough against the edge of a table or desk to make two roughly equal pieces. Place both pieces on the wax paper.

EARTH SCIENCE

Dough Fault of Your Own, continued

18. Holding one piece in place, press and slide the other piece on the tabletop along the direction of the crack. Does the dough slide smoothly as you push or does it stick?

_____

_____

_____

19. How is the rock motion along a transverse fault during an earthquake similar to the motion you modeled in step 18?

_____

_____

_____

_____

_____

Rocks on the Slide

20. Remove both parts of Stack B from the freezer. Unwrap the two pieces and place them flat on the table so that the cut ends touch one another. Without allowing the dough to warm, push the two pieces together. The pieces slide against one another. Describe the placement of the two pieces.

_____

_____

_____

21. How is the movement of rocks along a reverse or thrust fault similar to this movement?

_____

_____

_____

_____

_____

Dough Fault of Your Own, continued

Critical Thinking

22. If the dough in Stack B were warmed to room temperature, would the pieces of your reverse-fault model be more likely to slide over one another or to bend and fold? Explain your answer.

_____

_____

_____

_____

23. Compare the behavior of the dough as it warms with the behavior of rocks as they are heated.

_____

_____

_____

_____

Now that you are done with your lab, slice your stacks into cookies! Place the cookies on an ungreased cookie sheet in an oven set at 400°F. Cook for 8–10 minutes.

EARTH SCIENCE

MAKING MODELS

Hot Spots

Cooperative Learning Activity

Group size: 3–5 students

Group goal: To use a model to study the development of an island chain over a geologic hot spot

Positive interdependence: Each group member should choose a role, such as map maker, whipped-cream sprayer, or observer.

Individual accountability: After the activity, each group member should be able to explain how an island chain forms over a hot spot and to identify the strengths and weaknesses in the model mentioned above.

Time Required

One 45-minute class period

Lab Ratings

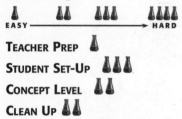

EASY ——→ HARD

TEACHER PREP
STUDENT SET-UP
CONCEPT LEVEL
CLEAN UP

Advance Preparation

Obtain copies (black-and-white or color) of a large map of the Hawaiian Islands that has a scale of at least 1:24,000. One such map is available from Map Link (ISBN 0-671-85050-4; phone: 1-805-692-6777; fax: 1-800-627-7768, online at www.maplink.com). Be sure to make enough copies so that there is one map for each student group. Each map should be about the size of a standard road map.

Provide enough cardboard for each student group to mount the map. To save time and materials, you may wish to mount, laminate, and punch holes in the maps in advance.

Be sure that the whipped-cream spray cans you use for this activity do not have

to be upside down to work properly. After the activity, you may wish to provide the class with some foods that can be eaten with whipped cream, such as fruit or poundcake.

Shaving cream makes an excellent substitute for whipped cream.

Safety Information

Whipped cream cans that do not use nitrous oxide are now widely available. Instruct students to avoid pointing the can nozzles at one another and to be mindful of how much whipped cream they spray. Students should exercise caution when using scissors.

Teaching Strategies

You may wish to review the basic principles of volcano formation and plate tectonics with students before beginning this activity.

Evaluation Strategies

For help evaluating this lab, see the Teacher Evaluation of Cooperative Group Activity in the *Assessment Checklists & Rubrics*. This checklist is also available in the *One-Stop Planner CD-ROM*.

Elizabeth Rustad
Crane Junior High
Yuma, Arizona

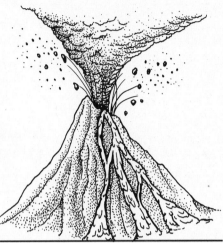

MAKING MODELS

Hot Spots

If you look at a map of the Hawaiian Islands, you might notice that the five main islands form a nearly straight line. That's no coincidence. The islands are part of the Pacific plate, which is gradually drifting northwest over a *hot spot*. As the plate moves over the hot spot, magma from the hot spot erupts through the crust, creating underwater volcanoes that eventually become islands. These islands are carried away from the hot spot like packages on a conveyer belt, creating the island chain we see today. In this lab, you will simulate the formation of a chain of volcanic islands by a hot spot.

MATERIALS

- map of the Hawaiian Islands
- glue stick
- piece of cardboard having the same dimensions as the map
- scissors
- metric ruler
- spray can of whipped cream

 Ask a Question

How did the Hawaiian Islands form from volcanoes generated by a hot spot?

Conduct an Experiment

1. Glue the map onto the cardboard. Allow the glue to dry.

2. Cut a hole about 1–2 cm in diameter in the map. The hole should be centered on the island of Hawaii.

3. Cut another hole in the map, this time on the island of Maui. Make sure this hole is at least 4 cm from the first hole.

4. Cut three more holes in the map on the three other main islands: Molokai, Oahu, and Kauai. Be sure that all the holes are spaced at least 4 cm apart.

5. Shake the can of whipped cream for a few seconds.

6. Move two small tables close together, leaving a gap of at least 5 cm between them.

7. Lay the map horizontally on the two tables so that the hole centered on the island of Hawaii is above the gap.

8. From under the map, have one group member spray a *small* amount of whipped cream through the hole while other group members watch from above. A small mound of whipped cream will slowly grow on the map surface. When the mound is about the circumference of a half-dollar, the group members who are watching should tell the other student to stop spraying.

9. Slowly slide the map horizontally so that the hole closest to the mound is above the gap between the tables.

EARTH SCIENCE

10. Pass the spray can to another student in the group, and re-peat steps 8–9 for the new hole.

11. Continue to repeat step 10. Be sure that every student in the group has a chance to build a whipped-cream mound.

12. After creating whipped-cream mounds over all five holes, pause to observe any changes occurring to the mounds. Then proceed to the discussion questions below.

Analyze the Results

13. What do the holes and the whipped cream represent?

_____

_____

_____

_____

_____

14. How did the whipped cream mounds change over time?

_____

_____

_____

15. What does this suggest about the relative ages of the five Hawaiian islands?

_____

_____

_____

Critical Thinking

16. What physical processes might be at work to cause these changes?

_____

_____

_____

_____

Draw Conclusions

17. Which of the five Hawaiian Islands you examined most likely still have active volcanoes? Explain your answer.

_____

_____

_____

_____

18. Assume that the Hawaiian hot spot is still active. Is it possible for a new volcano to form another Hawaiian island? Explain your answer.

_____

_____

_____

_____

_____

19. Identify two weaknesses of using whipped cream to represent the magma that formed the Hawaiian volcanoes.

_____

_____

_____

_____

_____

_____

Going Further

Not all volcanic islands are created by hot spots. Many, like the Aleutian Islands, form over convergent plate boundaries. Others, like Iceland's island of Surtsey, form over divergent plate boundaries. Design an experiment to demonstrate how one of these other types of volcanic islands form.

EARTH SCIENCE

DISCOVERY LAB

Meteorite Delight

Purpose

Students compare meteorite finds and falls to determine why iron meteorites are found with greater frequency than stony meteorites.

Time Required

One 45-minute class period

Lab Ratings

EASY ————————→ HARD

TEACHER PREP

STUDENT SET-UP

CONCEPT LEVEL

CLEAN UP

Advance Preparation

Prepare a batch of rice-cereal balls according to the recipe on page 81, or have students make the rice balls. If you choose to have students prepare the rice balls, be sure to warn them to be very careful when they are near the burner or oven.

Stony meteorites will be modeled with plain rice cereal, and iron meteorites will be modeled with cocoa-flavored rice cereal. Each student group will need 12 plain rice-cereal balls and 2 cocoa-flavored rice-cereal balls.

You may wish to provide additional rice-cereal balls for students to eat after completing the activity.

Teaching Strategies

This activity requires that students work in groups of at least two. Remind students to make their observations of falling "meteorites" from across the room or hallway. Students should clean up any spilled rice cereal and discard it in a trash can.

Background Information

Share the following information with students *before beginning* the activity:

Meteors are small pieces of rock and metal in outer space. A meteor that falls to Earth is called a meteorite. There are three types of meteorites: stony, iron, and stony-iron. Stony meteorites contain materials similar to the substances that make up rocks on Earth. Iron meteorites have a shiny, metallic appearance. Stony-iron meteorites contain a combination of stony and iron materials. They are extremely rare and therfore will not be considered in this activity.

Once students know the three types of meteorites, explain the difference between a find and a fall. A *find* is a meteorite that was found on the ground but was not seen falling to the ground. A *fall* is a meteorite that was tracked as it fell to the ground and was then recovered.

Share the following information with the class as a summary *after completing* the activity:

Stony meteorites are the most common kinds of meteorites, but they are hard to find on the ground because they closely resemble Earth's own rocks. Iron meteorites fall less frequently, but they have a unique appearance and are therefore easier to locate on the ground.

continued...

Brian Burnight
Big Bear Middle School
Big Bear Lake, California

The distinction between finds and falls is important. When scientists count the number of finds, they are bound to overlook a significant number of stony meteorites. An analysis of the number of falls is likely to be more accurate, however, since the same number of iron and stony meteorites are likely to be tracked and recovered. Falls more closely reflect the distribution of meteorites in space than finds do. When scientists analyze the meteorites that they discover, they find that about 90 percent of the falls are stony while only about 30 percent of the finds are stony.

Craters often form when massive meteorites strike the Earth. The presence of a crater aids scientists in recovering meteorites. However, most meteorites have a mass of less than 1 kg and do not form craters.

Evaluation Strategies

For help evaluating this lab, see the Activity Observation Checklist in the *Assessment Checklists & Rubrics*. This checklist is also available in the *One-Stop Planner CD-ROM*.

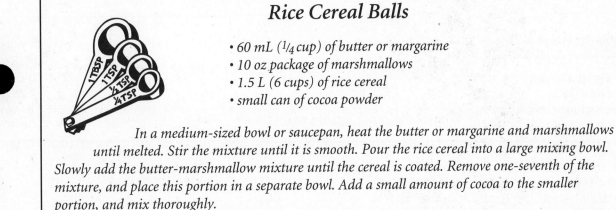

Rice Cereal Balls

- 60 mL (¹/₄ cup) of butter or margarine
- 10 oz package of marshmallows
- 1.5 L (6 cups) of rice cereal
- small can of cocoa powder

In a medium-sized bowl or saucepan, heat the butter or margarine and marshmallows until melted. Stir the mixture until it is smooth. Pour the rice cereal into a large mixing bowl. Slowly add the butter-marshmallow mixture until the cereal is coated. Remove one-seventh of the mixture, and place this portion in a separate bowl. Add a small amount of cocoa to the smaller portion, and mix thoroughly.

Allow both mixtures to cool for 5–7 minutes. Then form the mixtures into small balls, and place the balls on a buttered baking dish or cookie sheet. Cover with plastic wrap, and refrigerate until cool.

This recipe makes about 42 balls.

EARTH SCIENCE

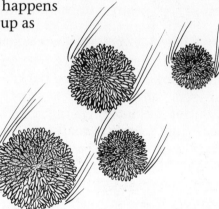

DISCOVERY
LAB

Meteorite Delight

Chunks of rock and metal race through space. What happens when they enter the Earth's atmosphere? Most burn up as they plummet, but some land on the ground. These objects are called *meteorites*. Meteorites come in two major forms: *stony,* which look similar to Earth rocks, and *iron,* which appear shiny and metallic.

There are two ways to discover meteorites. A meteorite *fall* occurs when someone sees the meteorite, traces its path to Earth, and recovers it. A meteorite *find* occurs when someone discovers a meteorite on the ground without having seen it fall.

In this activity, you will work in groups of two or more students to simulate the impact of stony and iron meteorites on the ground. Rice-cereal balls will serve as meteorites to help you better understand meteorite finds and falls.

MATERIALS

- large baking pan or cookie sheet
- box of plain puffed rice cereal
- 12 plain rice-cereal balls
- 2 cocoa-flavored rice cereal balls

Ask a Question

How do meteorite finds differ from meteorite falls?

Conduct an Experiment

1. Fill the baking pan with puffed rice cereal. Smooth the top of the cereal so that it is level with the top of the pan. Then place 10 of the rice-cereal balls without cocoa across the top of the pan.

2. Place the pan at one end of the classroom. Decide who will drop the cereal balls and who will make observations. The person who drops the cereal balls should stand next to the pan while the observer stands across the room.

3. To conduct the first trial, hold a plain rice-cereal ball (representing a stony meteorite) at shoulder height directly above the pan. While the observer is watching, drop the ball.

4. The observer should then examine the pan and identify which ball was just dropped. Record in the "Observed" columns of the Meteorite Observation Chart, on page 83, whether the meteorite was correctly identified.

5. Repeat steps 3–4 with another plain rice-cereal ball and with two cocoa-flavored rice balls (representing iron meteorites), dropping the balls one at a time.

Meteorite Observation Chart

Trial	Observed		Not observed	
	Meteorite was identified correctly	Meteorite was not identified correctly	Meteorite was identified correctly	Meteorite was not identified correctly
Student 1— Trial 1: plain				
Trial 2: plain				
Trial 3: cocoa				
Trial 4: cocoa				
Student 2— Trial 5: plain				
Trial 6: plain				
Trial 7: cocoa				
Trial 8: cocoa				

6. Switch roles, and repeat steps 1–5. Record the results of all of your observations in the Meteorite Observation Chart.

7. Repeat steps 1–6, except this time the student who is not dropping the balls should NOT observe them dropping. Record your findings in the "Not observed" column of the Meteorite Observation Chart.

Analyzing the Results

8. What did the following parts of the model represent?

   a. plain rice-cereal balls that were dropped

   _____

   b. plain rice-cereal balls that were placed on the layer of rice

   cereal _____

   c. rice cereal _____

   d. cocoa rice-cereal balls _____

9. Were your first set of trials representative of meteorite finds or meteorite falls? Explain.

   _____

   _____

EARTH SCIENCE

Meteorite Delight, continued

10. Was your second set of trials representative of meteorite finds or meteorite falls? Explain.

_____

_____

_____

11. Which kind of meteorite were you more likely to identify correctly? Explain.

_____

_____

_____

12. Other than the appearance of the meteorite, identify another way to determine whether a rock is a meteorite find or an Earth rock. (Hint: Consider what happened to the puffed-rice cereal when you dropped a rice ball.)

_____

_____

_____

Critical Thinking

13. Should scientists base their predictions about the number of stony or iron meteorites that exist in outer space on finds or on falls? Explain your reasoning.

_____

_____

_____

Going Further

While a few meteorites are extremely massive and leave craters for scientists to analyze, most meteorites are smaller than a pea. Find out how scientists study these meteorites. Are they more likely to discover tiny meteorites in finds or in falls?

How Cold Is Ice-Cream Cold?

Cooperative Learning Activity

Group size: 3–4 students

Group goal: To investigate the effects of a solute on the freezing point of a solvent

Positive interdependence: Each group member should choose a role, such as ice-cream maker, recorder, ice-cream tester, or materials coordinator.

Individual accountability: After the activity, each group member should be able to explain how salt affected the temperature and freezing point of water.

Time Required

One 45-minute class period

Lab Ratings

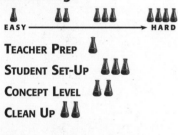

EASY ——————————→ HARD

TEACHER PREP

STUDENT SET-UP

CONCEPT LEVEL

CLEAN UP

Advance Preparation

The cream mixture should be made a day in advance and stored overnight in the refrigerator. The recipe on this page produces about fifteen 240 mL (1 cup) portions of ice cream. Mix all of the ingredients well.

Label half the large plastic bags "Salt," and label the other half "No Salt." If you wish, you can reuse the large bags to limit the bags that need to be purchased.

You will need to have ice cubes available for this activity. If an ice-cube maker is unavailable, you may wish to purchase a bag of ice from a local grocery store.

ADDITIONAL MATERIALS

- 1.9 L ($\frac{1}{2}$ gal) of milk
- 1.9 L ($\frac{1}{2}$ gal) of whipping cream
- 0.70–0.95 L (3–4 cup) of sugar
- 10 mL (2 tsp) of vanilla

Safety Information

Caution students that ice and salt bags can become very cold; they can reach temperatures as low as −21°C! Students should wear gloves or mittens when shaking the bag.

Teaching Strategies

If students are having difficulty, you may wish to share some of the following background information as they perform the activity.

Background Information

Ice cream is made by surrounding cream with a very cold solution of water, salt, and ice. The temperature of the solution is lowered in the following two ways:

- First, adding salt to water causes the temperature of the water to decrease. Temperature is a measure of how fast the molecules in a substance are moving. The more energetic the motion is, the higher the temperature will be. When salt is dissolved in water, the separated sodium and chlorine ions that make up the salt molecules absorb energy from the water. As the energy is absorbed, the water molecules move more slowly, and the temperature of the solution decreases.

continued...

Donna Norwood
Monroe Middle School
Charlotte, North Carolina

PHYSICAL SCIENCE

• Second, adding ice to water causes the temperature of the water to decrease. When ice and water are placed in the same container, some of the water freezes into ice, and some of the ice melts into water.

At the freezing point of water, 0°C, these two processes occur at the same rate. At higher temperatures, the ice melts faster than the water freezes, so eventually all of the ice melts. At lower temperatures, the water freezes faster than the ice melts, so eventually all of the water freezes.

The salt and the ice also work together to lower the temperature of the water; the sodium and chloride ions from the salt tend to block the water molecules from attaching to ice crystals and refreezing. The water then freezes at a slower rate than it melts, making it possible for the liquid water to become even colder—and closer to the actual temperature of the ice.

The expected temperature drop for a salt-water solution with a ratio of 1:3 is about 5°C. The mixture used to make ice cream in this activity freezes at about −3°C, which is higher than the temperature of most home freezers but lower than the temperature of a glass of ice water. Emphasize that ice water without salt is not cold enough to freeze ice cream.

Evaluation Strategies

For help evaluating this lab, see the Group Evaluation for Cooperative Group Activity in the *Assessment Checklists & Rubrics.* This checklist is also available in the *One-Stop Planner CD-ROM.*

Name _____ Date _____ Class _____

SKILL BUILDER

How Cold Is Ice-Cream Cold?

Have you ever heard the expression "cold as water"? Probably not. That's because ice can get much colder than 0°C, the freezing point of water. When something is really cold, it's "cold as ice."

But there is a way to make water colder than 0°C without freezing it: just add salt! In this lab, you will explore the effects of a solute—something that dissolves—on the temperature and freezing point of a liquid. And you will make delicious ice cream in the process.

MATERIALS

- 2 beakers, 250 mL each, labeled "Salt" and "No Salt"
- waterproof marker for labeling
- water
- 2 thermometers that measure to −20°C
- 480 g of rock salt
- watch or clock that indicates seconds
- 230 mL of cream mixture
- 4 small (20 × 20 cm) resealable plastic bags
- 2 large (30 × 30 cm) resealable plastic bags, labeled "Salt" and "No Salt"
- 2 pairs of mittens or gloves
- 800 mL of small ice chips
- graduated cylinder
- freezer

Ask a Question

What is the effect of a solute on the temperature and freezing point of ice water?

Make Observations

1. Fill the 250 mL beakers with 200 mL of water. Measure the temperature of the water in the "No Salt" beaker, and record your results in the chart below.

2. Add 80 g of rock salt to the "Salt" beaker, and stir until the salt is completely dissolved. Measure the temperature of the water and record.

3. After 2 minutes, measure and record the temperature of the water in each beaker. Be sure to clean the thermometer after each measurement.

4. Repeat step 3 until the temperature no longer changes. Record the total temperature change, if any, for each beaker.

Water Temperature Data Chart

Temp (°C)	No salt	Salt
Initial		
2 minutes		
4 minutes		
6 minutes		
Total change		

5. What happened to the temperature of the water in the "No Salt" beaker?

_____

_____

_____

6. What happened to the temperature of the water with added salt?

_____

_____

_____

7. Why do you think the salt had this effect on the water?

_____

_____

_____

Make a Prediction

8. If you dissolve salt in ice water, what do you think will happen to the temperature of the water?

_____

_____

_____

_____

Conduct an Experiment

9. Divide the cream mixture evenly between two small bags. Force any extra air from each bag as you carefully seal it.

10. Place each cream mixture bag into a second small bag, and seal the second bags.

11. Place one double-bagged cream portion into each of the labeled large bags. The student holding each bag should now put on mittens or gloves.

12. Add 400 mL of ice chips and 100 mL of water to each large bag.

13. After 1 minute, measure the temperature of the ice water in each bag by inserting the thermometer bulbs into the water at the bottom of the bags. Record the temperatures in the Temperature Data Table on page 90.

14. Pour the rock salt over the ice in the bag labeled "Salt." Seal both bags carefully.

15. Shake the bags gently for 5 minutes to mix and chill the contents. You may choose to roll the bags back and forth on a desk or tabletop. Be careful not to break the seals on the bags!

16. Carefully open one end of the sealed "No Salt" bag, and insert the thermometer into the water at the bottom of the bag. Record the temperature, and reseal the bag.

17. Repeat the procedure in step 16 for the "Salt" bag.

18. Repeat steps 15–17 twice.

19. Reach into the "Salt" bag, and test the consistency of the cream mixture. If the mixture is still liquid, repeat steps 15–17. If the mixture has begun to solidify, record the temperature and note it as the freezing point in the Data Table. Remove the cream packets from both bags, and place the packets in the freezer to harden.

20. Discard the liquid, salt, and ice in the sink.

Analyze the Results

Look over your results on the chart.

21. What was the lowest temperature reached?

In the bag without salt? _____

In the bag with salt? _____

22. Was your prediction from step 8 correct? Explain.

_____

_____

_____

_____

_____

_____

_____

PHYSICAL SCIENCE

Temperature Data Table

Time (min)	Salt		No salt	
	Temperature (°C)	Cream consistency	Temperature (°C)	Cream consistency
0				
5				
10				
15				
20				

23. How did the salt affect the freezing point of water?

_____

_____

Critical Thinking

24. Use your results from step 23 to explain how ice on a side-walk melts when salt is spread on it, even though the temperature of the ice remains below 0°C, the freezing point of water.

_____

_____

_____

_____

_____

DISCOVERY LAB

An Iron-ic Cereal Experience

Purpose

Students extract iron from a breakfast cereal to explore the difference between a mixture containing metallic iron and an iron compound.

Time Required

One 45-minute class period

Lab Ratings

EASY ——————————→ HARD

TEACHER PREP 🍾🍾
STUDENT SET-UP 🍾
CONCEPT LEVEL 🍾🍾
CLEAN UP 🍾🍾

Advance Preparation

You will need to make 20 magnetic stirring rods for this activity. For each stirring rod, place a magnet near one end of a pencil and attach the magnet with tape. Place each pencil-magnet assembly in the bottom of a sandwich bag, and seal the bag.

The cereal used in this lab must be iron-fortified. In iron supplements, three capsules typically contain 18 mg of iron, which is the recommended daily allowance (RDA) set by the government.

ADDITIONAL MATERIALS

- roll of waterproof electrical tape
- 20 small magnets, 1–2 cm in diameter
- 20 sealable plastic sandwich bags
- 20 pencils, slightly shorter than the width of the bags

Teaching Strategies

This activity works best in groups of 2–3 students. Begin the activity by showing students a box of nails and telling them, "I found this in my cereal this morning!"

Background Information

You may also wish to discuss the difference between a mixture and a compound. This distinction is important when considering the absorption of iron by our bodies. Iron is most readily used by the body when it is in a compound, such as ferrous sulfate, ferrous fumarate, or ferrous gluconate. The iron in many dietary supplements is in compound form.

Unfortunately, this form of iron also tends to oxidize when it is exposed to air, and oxidized iron is unusable. Iron that is mixed into certain fortified breakfast cereals is in a metallic state because metallic iron does not oxidize as easily. The metallic iron is converted to a ferrous compound by the hydrochloric acid in the stomach, where it is then absorbed by the body.

Evaluation Strategies

For help evaluating this lab, see the Rubric for Performance Assessment in the *Assessment Checklists & Rubrics*.

 This rubric is also available in the *One-Stop Planner CD-ROM*.

CLASSROOM TESTED & APPROVED

Cherrill Stephenson
Sun Valley Middle School
Sun Valley, California

PHYSICAL SCIENCE

LAB
19 **STUDENT WORKSHEET**

DISCOVERY
LAB

An Iron-ic Cereal Experience

You have probably walked down the cereal aisle in a supermarket and seen the phrase "fortified with iron" on many of the boxes. That means iron has been added to the cereal. Have you ever wondered why?

Well, iron helps to carry oxygen to different parts of your body. Green leafy vegetables are great sources of iron, but iron-fortified cereals are too!

How could you find out if there is iron in your cereal? One way you can tell is by using a magnet! Iron is found in two forms: as an element and as part of a compound.

Elemental iron is attracted to magnets, while iron in a compound form is not. If the cereal contains elemental iron, the iron can be extracted with the magnet.

MATERIALS

- 2 magnetic stirring rods, each in a small plastic bag
- small amount of iron filings
- 90 g of iron-fortified cereal
- 1 L graduated cylinder
- 500 mL beakers (2)
- water
- 3 dietary iron capsules
- watch or clock

USEFUL TERMS

elemental iron
iron in its pure state

compound
a substance made up of atoms of at least two different elements held together by chemical bonds

SCIENTIFIC
METHOD

Ask a Question

How can a magnet be used to explore the difference between elemental iron and an iron compound?

Conduct an Experiment

1. Move one of the stirring rods close to the iron filings. What happens?

_____

_____

_____

2. What does this tell you about the iron in the filings?

_____

_____

_____

3. Remove the filings from the outside of the bag, and discard them.

An Iron-ic Cereal Experience, continued

4. Thoroughly crush the cereal. Place the cereal in the first beaker, and add 100 mL of water. Set the beaker aside.

5. Empty the contents of the iron capsules into the second beaker, and add 100 mL of water. Set the second beaker aside.

6. Roll up the bags containing the stirring rods so that they are easier to hold. After the cereal has become soggy (10–15 minutes), use a stirring rod, magnet side down, to slowly stir the contents of each beaker for 5 minutes.

7. Carefully remove both stirring rods, and examine them closely.

Analyze the Results

8. What did you see on the stirring rod from the first beaker?

_____

_____

_____

9. What did you see on the stirring rod from the second beaker?

_____

_____

_____

Draw Conclusions

10. Based on these observations and what you know about the appearance of iron filings, do you think elemental iron is present in one or both of the beakers? Explain your answer.

_____

_____

_____

_____

_____

_____

PHYSICAL SCIENCE

11. What form of iron was in the capsules? Explain your answer.

_____

_____

_____

_____

12. If you dip a magnetic stirring rod in the cereal and no iron sticks to the rod, does that mean there is no iron in the cereal? Explain your answer.

_____

_____

_____

_____

_____

_____

Going Further

Find out what the terms *fortified* and *enriched* mean when they appear on nutritional food labels.

DISCOVERY LAB

Power-Packed Peanuts

Cooperative Learning Activity

Group size: 2–3 students

Group goal: To determine the amount of energy that is stored in a peanut and released during oxidation

Positive interdependence: Each group member should choose a role, such as chief experimenter, materials and safety manager, or recorder.

Individual responsibility: Each group member should be able to write a self-assessment describing what he or she contributed to the group, how well he or she worked with the group, and what he or she learned by performing the experiment.

Time Required

One 45-minute class period

Lab Ratings

EASY ———————→ HARD

TEACHER PREP ▲▲
STUDENT SET-UP ▲▲
CONCEPT LEVEL ▲▲
CLEAN UP ▲▲

Advance Preparation

The week before the lab, ask a few students to bring clean 12 oz juice or soda cans to class. Butane lighters may be substituted for matches. If there are no clamps available for the thermometers, students can hold the thermometers as they check the water temperature.

Safety Information

Students should always be careful around an open flame. Make sure students tie back loose hair and secure loose clothing. Students who are allergic to nuts should not eat the peanuts.

Teaching Strategies

You may need to remind students that the mass of 1 mL of water is 1 g.

Students can also determine the number of nutritional calories in a peanut. Nutritional calories are equal to kilocalories, or Calories, defined as the amount of thermal energy needed to raise 1000 mL of water 1°C. One Calorie equals 4.184 kJ or 4184 J. To calculate nutritional calories, students should divide the number of joules by a conversion factor of 4,184.

Background Information

You may wish to share the following background information with students: Peanuts contain proteins, fats, and complex carbohydrates. Oxidation of the molecular bonds in these foods leads to the release of a significant amount of energy. Oxidation through burning the peanut is one way to release the energy stored in the peanut. In this activity, students will measure the amount of energy released by the burning peanut by monitoring the temperature change as water is heated.

Evaluation Strategies

 For help evaluating this lab, see the Self Evaluation of Cooperative Group Activity in the *Assessment Checklists & Rubrics*. This checklist is also available in the *One-Stop Planner CD-ROM*.

Randy Christian
Stovall Junior High
Houston, Texas

PHYSICAL SCIENCE

LAB
20 **STUDENT WORKSHEET**

DISCOVERY LAB

Power-Packed Peanuts

The world runs on many different kinds of fuel—cars run on gas, and our homes are often heated by oil. But did you know you can burn a peanut to heat water? A peanut may be small, but this amazing underground fruit can pack quite a punch! Let's take a look at just how much energy we can find in a peanut.

MATERIALS

- alcohol thermometer
- support stand with ring clamp
- wire gauze
- clean, empty can
- shelled peanut
- paper clip
- cork covered in aluminum foil
- metric ruler
- 125 mL graduated cylinder
- water
- matches

SCIENTIFIC **METHOD**

Ask a Question

How do you measure the amount of energy in a peanut?

Conduct an Experiment

1. Set up the apparatus as shown below. Be sure to place the thermometer so that the tip is in the can but does not touch the bottom of the can. The can should be 2.5–5 cm from the top of the peanut.

2. Pour 100 mL of water into the can, and record the water temperature in the Temperature Chart on page 97.

3. Light a match, and set fire to the peanut. **Caution:** Be careful not to burn yourself.

4. When the flame goes out, monitor the water temperature until it no longer changes. Record your measurements in the Temperature Chart on page 97, and then calculate the increase in temperature.

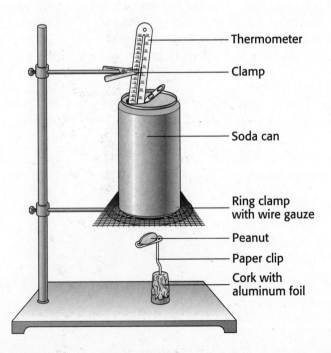

- Thermometer
- Clamp
- Soda can
- Ring clamp with wire gauze
- Peanut
- Paper clip
- Cork with aluminum foil

Temperature Chart

Water temperature before heating:	_____	°C
Water temperature after heating:	_____	°C
Temperature increase:	_____	°C

Analyze the Results

5. Calculate the energy in the peanut, measured in joules, by calculating the energy absorbed by the water. Use the following formula:

joules = mass of the water × temperature increase × 4.2 J/(g°C)

Show your work.

_____

_____

_____

_____

Critical Thinking

6. Explain why the results obtained from using this apparatus can be inaccurate.

_____

_____

_____

_____

_____

_____

_____

_____

Critical Thinking

7. How could the results of the experiment be improved?

_____

_____

_____

_____

_____

8. How would you measure the energy content of milk? Explain your answer.

_____

_____

_____

_____

_____

_____

Going Further

Use your measuring device to test different nuts, such as pecans, walnuts, and sunflower seeds. How does their energy content compare with that of a peanut?

Now You're Cooking!

Cooperative Learning Activity

Group size: 3–4 students

Group goal: To demonstrate how to efficiently collect and use solar energy by building a solar cooker.

Positive interdependence: Each group member should choose a role, such as recorder, discussion leader, research coordinator, or materials coordinator.

Individual accountability: After the contest, each group member should be able to discuss what worked and what didn't work in the research, design, and performance stages of this project.

Time Required

Four to six 45-minute periods
A suggested pacing guide is provided on page 100.

Lab Ratings

EASY ———————→ HARD

TEACHER PREP
STUDENT SET-UP
CONCEPT LEVEL
CLEAN UP

Advance Preparation

Before beginning this project, you may wish to review the principles of reflection and absorption of radiant energy with students. Mention that dark and matte surfaces tend to absorb the sun's rays, while shiny and light surfaces tend to reflect them.

Choose a date, time, and location for the contest. The class will need two days outside—one for testing and one for the cook-off. To ensure adequate space and sunlight, consider locations such as an open field or a parking lot. Be sure to choose a rain date in case of inclement weather. Keep in mind that this activity works well at lunch time! Allow for cooking time of up to an hour.

Distribute copies of the lab to students the day before they begin the lab. Give them the opportunity to read through the lab and come to class with questions.

You may need to schedule time in the library for students to conduct their research. To shorten research time, prepare a website bibliography or compile information on solar cookers that you can distribute to students.

You may wish to have additional pre-cooked hot dogs available for students to enjoy after the activity.

Safety Information

Students should use extreme caution when using sharp objects, such as scissors and cooking thermometers. Goggles should be worn when working with sharp objects. Students should wear goggles and aprons while cooking. Oven mitts should be worn when handling hot materials. Caution students not to touch hot thermometer probes after cooking. Analyze cooker designs and advise students on modifications needed for safe operation and handling.

continued...

CLASSROOM TESTED & APPROVED

Jane Lemons
Western Rockingham
Middle School
Madison, North Carolina

PHYSICAL SCIENCE

Teaching Strategies

Encourage students to be resourceful and thrifty in choosing materials. Ensure contest fairness by limiting the supplies budget for each team to $5, and by supplying students with identical thermometers and hot dogs. The thermometers should have a dial and should be able to measure the internal temperature of the hot dog to at least 100°C.

Before students begin their design phase, clearly communicate the contest rules. You may wish to add your own rules to the following:

CONTEST RULES

- Do not touch anyone else's cooker.
- No electricity or flames may be used.
- All teams will wait for the teacher's signal to begin cooking.

Once all of the teams have finished cooking, encourage a class discussion to evaluate each cooker design.

Evaluation Strategies

 For help evaluating this lab, see the Rubric for Technology Projects in the *Assessment Checklists & Rubrics*. This rubric is also available in the *One-Stop Planner CD-ROM*.

Suggested Pacing Guide

Days 1–2	Days 3–4	Day 5	Day 6
Research	**Testing and construction**	**The Great Solar Cook-Off!**	**Evaluation**
Class divided into teams of 3–4. Each team member chooses a role.	Students gather materials and begin construction of approved solar cooker designs.	The team whose cooker heats the hot dog to 100°C first wins.	Class discussion to evaluate the performance and results of each team's cooker.
Students brainstorm ideas, and begin research.	Completed cookers are tested, adjusted, and retested as needed.		Students evaluate team progress and results independently.
Students finish research, discuss and evaluate findings, and chose one cooker design.	Students prepare for cook-off.		
Each team submits a proposal and materials list to teacher for approval.			

LAB 21 **STUDENT WORKSHEET**

DESIGN YOUR OWN

Now You're Cooking!

Have you ever walked barefoot across a black surface on a hot summer day? Ouch! The black surface gets much hotter than the air around you because the surface is an effective absorber of the sun's rays, or solar energy. The pavement absorbs solar energy and stores it as thermal energy.

Solar energy can be used to cook other things besides your feet. In this project, you will be part of a team that will compete to build the best solar energy collector for cooking a hot dog. The winning cooker will be the first one to raise the internal temperature of a hot dog to 100°C. The planning and construction of the cooker is up to you, so put your hot ideas to work!

MATERIALS

- boxes with removable tops
- reflective emergency blanket
- oven cooking bag
- aluminum foil
- newspaper
- white glue
- scissors
- masking tape
- pen or marker
- metric ruler
- 2 oven mitts
- cooking thermometer
- 2 hot dogs or other food items
- hot dog buns, mustard, relish, etc.

Ask a Question

What kind of solar cooker will most effectively heat a hot dog to 100°C?

Brainstorm

As a team, determine how you will solve the above problem. Ask yourself questions such as the following:

- What size and shape should your cooker be in order to collect sunlight most effectively?

- What is the best way to trap thermal energy in the cooker?

- Should you include a lid in the design?

- How will different materials, colors, thicknesses, and textures affect your cooker's performance?

- Will you need to adjust your cooker as the position of the sun changes?

- Will your cooker work well in partial sunlight?

Form a Hypothesis

Based on your discussion, record a hypothesis in your ScienceLog about what kind of solar cooker will best accomplish your goal.

PHYSICAL SCIENCE

Name _____ Date _____ Class _____

Project Checklist for Now You're Cooking!

COLLECT DATA

___ 1. **Research solar cookers.** Consult periodicals, the Internet, and encyclopedias to learn about various types of solar cookers. Pay special attention to how each cooker works and how each was constructed.

___ 2. **Discuss your research.** Present your research to your team. Tell about the important components of each possible design, including the methods of collecting radiant energy and retaining thermal energy. Discuss the pros and cons of how each design collects radiant energy and retains thermal energy. Discuss how simple or complex each cooker will be to build.

___ 3. **Develop your design.** Decide which solar cooker design you want to use. You may decide to combine elements from several of the cookers researched or use your own ideas to improve a cooker design. Make sure that your design includes a thermometer inside the cooker that will be readable from the outside.

___ 4. **Write a design proposal.** Provide input to the recorder, who will write a short report describing how your solar cooker will work and explaining why your team chose this particular design.

___ 5. **Create a materials list.** Provide input to your materials coordinator so that he or she can generate a supplies list and attach it to the proposal.

___ 6. **Submit your team's proposal to the teacher for approval.**

DATE DUE: _____

___ 7. **Gather your materials.** After your design is approved, your materials coordinator should assign each team member specific items to obtain.

CONDUCT AN
EXPERIMENT

___ 8. **Build the cooker.** Begin construction of the cooker. Each team member should have a specific task in the process.

___ 9. **Test your design.** Your recorder should keep track of the time it takes to heat the hot dog to 100°C.

___ 10. **Adjust/modify your design.** Discuss your test results and evaluate any problems in the design. Make the necessary adjustments to improve the cooker.

Project Checklist for Now You're Cooking! continued

___ **11. Compete in the Great Solar Cook-Off!** Have your thermo-meter and hot dog ready to go. Carefully push the thermometer point lengthwise through the end of the hot dog so that the tip is centered in the hot dog. Ask your teacher to check your hot dog-thermometer assembly.

On your teacher's signal, place the hot dog in the cooker, making sure that you can still read the thermometer. Your recorder will note the temperature every 5 minutes. As soon as the thermometer reads 100°C, the recorder should record the time and notify your teacher immediately.

ANALYZE THE
RESULTS

___ **12. Evaluate you solar cooker.** Once your hot dog is cooked, evaluate your cooker's performance. What worked? What didn't? How easy was your cooker to transport and set up? How expensive and available were the materials? How does you final design compare with the one described in your initial hypothesis? Record your notes in your ScienceLog.

COMMUNICATE
RESULTS

___ **13. Communicate what you learned.** Each group member should write a Research and Design report in his or her ScienceLog. Some questions to consider:

- How long did it take to cook the hot dog?

- What surprised you?

- What problems developed, and why didn't you find the problems in your initial testing?

- What worked and what didn't work in the creation and operation of the cooker?

- How did your cooker compare in operation and appear-ance with other cookers from the class?

- If you could, how would you change your design or ap-proach to the project?

- How does this cooking method compare with others?

___ **14. Turn your report in to your teacher.**

DATE DUE: _____

Baked Alaska

Purpose

Students explore the insulating property of meringue.

Time Required

20 minutes, at home

Lab Ratings

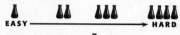

EASY ———————→ HARD

TEACHER PREP
STUDENT SET-UP
CONCEPT LEVEL
CLEAN UP

Advance Preparation

No advance preparation is necessary.

Safety Information

Remind students to wear oven mitts when using an oven.

Teaching Strategies

This lab makes an excellent at-home activity. Before assigning the lab to students, you may wish to perform it yourself at home.

Begin by asking students if they think they can bake ice cream without its melting. Ask them to explain their answers. Explain that in this activity they will have an opportunity to do so.

Background Information

You may wish to discuss with the class the three principal methods of heating. Point out that thermal energy can be transferred by *conduction, convection,* or *radiation.* In conduction, vibrating molecules pass energy to other vibrating molecules by direct contact. In convection, energy is carried by a moving fluid. In radiation, energy is carried by electromagnetic waves. Ask students to consider these different methods of heating as they make their baked Alaska. After students complete the activity, have them discuss which heating method kept the ice cream from melting.

Evaluation Strategies

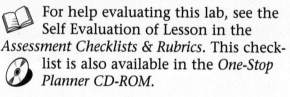 For help evaluating this lab, see the Self Evaluation of Lesson in the *Assessment Checklists & Rubrics.* This checklist is also available in the *One-Stop Planner CD-ROM.*

Donna Norwood
Monroe Middle School
Charlotte, North Carolina

LAB
22 **STUDENT WORKSHEET**

DISCOVERY LAB

Baked Alaska

Is it possible to bake ice cream without its melting? If you put a bowl of ice cream in a hot oven, you know what you'll get—ice cream soup! But what do you suppose would happen if you covered the ice cream with another food and then baked it? Let's find out.

MATERIALS

- conventional oven
- small bowl
- fork or wire whisk
- egg
- large spoonful of sugar (about 15 mL)
- pinch of salt
- electric mixer
- 2 large slices of sponge cake, pound cake, or angel food cake (10 cm square bread slices are also acceptable)
- cookie sheet covered with aluminum foil
- your favorite jam
- large spoon
- ice
- watch or clock
- oven mitts

Objective

To investigate the insulating property of meringue

Putting It Together

1. Preheat the oven to 250°C (475°F).

2. Prepare the meringue by cracking the egg and carefully separating the white from the yolk into a bowl. Discard the yolk. Beat the egg white with the fork or whisk until it holds its shape. Add the sugar and a pinch of salt, and then beat the mixture rapidly until it becomes very stiff. This is your meringue.

3. Put the two slices of cake on the cookie sheet. Spread a spoonful of jam over each slice of cake.

4. Get the ice cream from the freezer. Put a scoop of ice cream about 5 cm in diameter in the center of each slice of cake. Smooth the meringue over only ONE of the two scoops of ice cream, covering it completely. Check all sides to make sure the ice cream is well covered. Do not cover the other scoop of ice cream so that you can compare what happens to a covered scoop and an uncovered scoop.

5. While wearing the oven mitts, place the cookie sheet in the oven on the middle rack. Bake the cakes for 3 to 5 minutes, until the meringue turns light brown.

6. Remove the cakes from the oven, and serve them immediately.

PHYSICAL SCIENCE

A Baked Surprise

7. What happened to the ice cream on each of the pieces of cake?

_____

_____

_____

_____

8. Why do you think this happened?

_____

_____

_____

_____

9. Why was it important to make sure that the scoop of ice cream was completely covered with the meringue?

_____

_____

_____

_____

Going Further

You can explore the insulating properties of other foods. Repeat the activity with different toppings on the ice cream. Find out which foods most effectively keep the ice cream frozen. Do you see a pattern? Explain your answer.

Can You Say Seviche?

Purpose

Students demonstrate the effects of acids on the physical characteristics of raw fish.

Time Required

Fifteen minutes the first day and 30 minutes the second day.

Lab Ratings

EASY ———————————→ HARD

TEACHER PREP
STUDENT SET-UP
CONCEPT LEVEL
CLEAN UP

Advance Preparation

This lab makes an excellent at-home activity. If you choose to assign the lab as an at-home activity, you may wish to perform it yourself at home first.

You will need access to a refrigerator for this activity. If using frozen fish, allow enough time for it to defrost in the refrigerator. Once the fish has defrosted, use it immediately. Divide the fish fillets into 60-g portions. Cut the fish fillets into cubes, roughly 2 × 2 cm each. Place the portions in disposable bowls on trays. Cover the bowls with plastic wrap, and refrigerate until class time.

Line one or two trash bins with plastic bags. Designate these bins as receptacles in which to dispose of the fish after completing the lab.

Safety Information

To avoid spoilage, properly freeze, defrost, and refrigerate the fish until needed. Sharp knives are safer than dull ones. Use a very sharp knife to cut the fish. Instruct students to thoroughly wash their hands before and after performing the activity. Because lime juice can burn the mucous membranes and raw fish can carry microbes, students should avoid touching their faces during the activity.

Teaching Strategies

If performed in class, this activity works best in groups of 3–4 students.

On the second day of the activity, provide a cooked sample (either broiled or steamed) of the food the students used on Day 1. Display several samples in bowls so that students can compare the heat-cooked fish to the acid-cooked fish. To prepare seviche after the lab is completed, add 30 g of finely chopped red onion, 1–2 springs of finely chopped cilantro or parsley, 1 chopped tomato, 0.5 g of white pepper, and 0.1 g of ground cayenne pepper to bowl A, and stir.

Evaluation Strategies

 For help evaluating this lab, see the Rubric for Performance Assessment in the *Assessment Checklists & Rubrics.*

This rubric is also available in the *One-Stop Planner CD-ROM.*

Tracy Jahn
Berkshire Junior High
Canaan, New York

PHYSICAL SCIENCE

LAB 23 **STUDENT WORKSHEET**

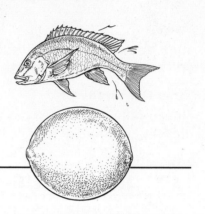

Can You Say Seviche?

You probably know that fish can be broiled, baked, fried, or grilled, but did you know that fish can also be *acid-cooked?* Seviche (suh-VEE-chay), a traditional Latin American dish, uses lime juice to prepare seafood, including fish, for eating. Lime is high in an acid called *citric acid*. The citric acid in the lime juice breaks down the proteins in the seafood, effectively cooking it without a stove or flame!

MATERIALS

- metric measuring spoon, 15 mL
- 60 mL of bottled lime juice
- 2 bowls, 250 mL or larger, labeled "A" and "B"
- tap water
- 60 g of white ocean fish fillets, raw, unbreaded, cubed
- 1 g of salt
- 2 plastic spoons
- plastic wrap
- refrigerator
- pH paper and scale, range 3–8

Objective

To observe the effects of acid on the physical characteristics of raw fish

Day 1: Lime Juice Meets Fish

1. Measure 60 mL of lime juice.

2. Pour the juice into bowl A. Rinse the measuring spoon well.

3. Measure an equal amount of tap water. Pour it into bowl B.

4. Describe the texture and appearance of the fish.

   _____

   _____

   _____

5. Place half the fish in bowl A and half in bowl B. Divide the salt in half, and sprinkle it over the fish in each bowl.

6. Use the spoon to mix the fish with the lime juice. Make sure the lime juice covers all of the fish cubes. Cover the bowl with plastic wrap. Rinse and dry the spoon.

7. Repeat step 6 for the fish in bowl B, substituting water for lime juice.

8. Place both bowls in the refrigerator as directed by your teacher. Be sure to label the two bowls that belong to your group.

Can You Say Seviche? continued

Day 2: Let's Sea the Results

9. Remove your bowls from the refrigerator, and uncover them.

10. Examine the fish in both bowls. Has the appearance of the fish in either bowl changed since yesterday? Describe any changes that you see.

_____

_____

_____

11. Using a different spoon for each sample, try to break the fish pieces apart. Describe the texture of the fish when you do this.

_____

_____

_____

_____

12. Compare the fish in bowls A and B with the bowls of cooked fish your teacher has provided. Which bowl of fish looks most like the heat-cooked fish?

_____

_____

13. What does this tell you about the effect of lime juice on fish?

_____

_____

Going Further

Around the world, many foods are prepared using a variety of edible acids. Use pH paper to test different foods in your house for acidity, and predict which substances might be used to "cook" food. Then research the cuisine of other cultures for recipes that employ acid-cooking. Identify the acids used in each recipe.

PHYSICAL SCIENCE

SKILL BUILDER

How To Fluff a Muffin

Purpose

Students learn how a reaction between an acid and a base causes muffins to rise.

Time Required

One 45-minute class period, or about 1 hour at home

Lab Ratings

EASY ————————————→ HARD

TEACHER PREP 🧪🧪🧪

STUDENT SET-UP 🧪🧪🧪

CONCEPT LEVEL 🧪🧪

CLEAN UP 🧪🧪

Advance Preparation

You will need a microwave oven for this activity. Make sure that there is an outlet and/or adapter to accommodate the microwave in your classroom. You will also need to create "muffin supports" from small paper cups. Do so by trimming the sides of each cup, leaving a 2.5 cm wall. Each student group will need one set of supports labeled 1–4. To determine the amount of dry mix and wet mix to prepare, multiply the quantities listed on this page by the number of groups.

To determine the baking time for a plate of muffins, you may wish to prepare a sample of batch #3 from page 111 the day before the experiment. Each group will cook a batch of four muffins, so choose a standard batch size of 8 or 12 muffins based on the size of the plate you are using. In a 650 watt microwave oven, six 50 mL samples of batter will cook in $1\frac{1}{2}$–$2\frac{1}{2}$ minutes. Bake for $1\frac{1}{2}$ minutes, then insert a wooden toothpick into the center of one of the muffins. If batter sticks to the toothpick, continue baking, and test the muffins again every 30 seconds. Note the total cooking time. Successful test batches can be brought to class.

The muffins that rise are edible. You may wish to have some additional edible muffins on hand for students to enjoy after the activity.

ADDITIONAL MATERIALS

Dry Mix
- 225 mL (1 cup) of flour
- 55 mL ($\frac{1}{4}$ cup) of sugar
- 1.2 mL ($\frac{1}{4}$ tsp) of salt

Wet mix
- 1 egg
- 55 mL ($\frac{1}{4}$ cup) of oil
- 55 mL ($\frac{1}{4}$ cup) of milk

Safety Information

Instruct students to allow muffins to cool before handling them. Students should use oven mitts or potholders when handling the hot plates.

Teaching Strategies

If performed in the classroom, this activity works best in groups of 3–4 students. Cream of tartar produces tartaric acid when moistened. This acid then reacts with baking soda ($NaHCO_3$), a base, to release carbon dioxide gas (CO_2). Heating also causes the baking soda to release carbon dioxide. The carbon dioxide forms bubbles in the batter that expand as the batter is heated, making the muffins light and fluffy. Baking powder, a common leavening agent, is made up of baking soda and tartaric acid. The acid and the base in baking powder do not interact until the powder is moistened.

Evaluation Strategies

 For help evaluating this lab, see the Rubric for Performance Assessment in the *Assessment Checklists & Rubrics*. This rubric is also available in the *One-Stop Planner* CD-ROM.

Donna Norwood
Monroe Middle School
Charlotte, North Carolina

SKILL
BUILDER

How To Fluff a Muffin

How do muffins rise in the morning? Like us, they usually need a little help. But instead of an alarm clock, like we use, they rely on a simple chemical reaction. Sodium bicarbonate (baking soda) and an acid combine to produce carbon dioxide gas. What would happen if you left these ingredients out? If you're not afraid of your experiment "falling flat," go ahead and try it!

MATERIALS

- 10 mL graduated cylinder
- water
- 2 test tubes, 10-15 mL each
- 1.2 mL ($\frac{1}{4}$ tsp) of baking soda (sodium bicarbonate)
- 0.6 mL ($\frac{1}{8}$ tsp) of cream of tartar (tartaric acid)
- 4 paper muffin liners
- 4 prelabeled muffin supports
- 100 mL beakers (4)
- 25 mL graduated cylinder
- 50 mL beakers (4)
- 4 forks
- microwavable plate
- microwave oven
- 2 oven mitts
- metric ruler

SCIENTIFIC
METHOD

Ask a Question

What are the effects of combining a base (sodium bicarbonate) with an acid (tartaric acid) in the making of muffins?

Make Observations

1. Measure 3 mL of water in the 10 mL graduated cylinder, and pour the water into a test tube.

2. Add the baking soda to the tube, and swirl the mixture. Describe what you see.

_____

_____

3. Add the cream of tartar to 3 mL of water in the second test tube, and swirl the mixture. What do you see?

_____

_____

4. Now pour the contents of the second tube (tartaric acid) into the first test tube. Describe and explain what happens.

_____

_____

PHYSICAL SCIENCE

Make a Prediction

5. In steps 1–3, you observed the effects of a chemical reaction involving baking soda, cream of tartar, and water. Now you will mix these three substances in various combinations into muffin batter to see how they affect the baking of muffins. Based on your observations from steps 1–3, predict what you think will happen to the muffins as they are baked.

_____

_____

_____

Conduct an Experiment

6. Number and label each paper muffin liner with the name of one person in your group. Place each liner in a support.

7. Each member of your team should mix one of the four batches given below by following these steps:

- Measure and level 40 mL of dry ingredients in a 50 mL beaker by tapping the beaker lightly on the desk. Pour the ingredients into a 100 mL beaker.

- For batches 1–3 only, measure baking soda and/or cream of tartar and mix with the dry ingredients using a fork.

- Make a well in the center of the dry mixture.

- Measure 22 mL of liquid mix in the 25 mL graduated cylinder, and pour the liquid into the well you made in the dry ingredients.

- Stir only enough to moisten the dry ingredients.

- Measure a beakerful of batter with a 50 mL beaker. Level off the batter by scraping the beaker with a fork, and pour the batter into the corresponding liner. Discard the remaining batter in a designated trash bag.

> For each batch:
> - 40 mL (2 tbsp + 2 tsp) of dry mix
> - 22 mL (1 tbsp + $1\frac{1}{2}$ tsp) of wet mix
>
> To batch #1 add:
> - 5 mL (1 tsp) of cream of tartar

How To Fluff A Muffin, continued

> To batch #2 add:
>
> • 1.8 mL ($\frac{3}{8}$ tsp) of baking soda
>
> To batch #3 add:
>
> • 5 mL (1 tsp) of cream of tartar
> • 1.8 mL ($\frac{3}{8}$ tsp) of baking soda
>
> To batch #4 add:
>
> • no additional ingredients

You are now ready to begin baking.

8. Keep all four samples together. Your teacher will coordinate the baking of the batter samples. Baking will take 1.5 to 2.5 minutes.

9. Once your muffins are baked and have cooled for 5 minutes, collect your group's samples.

10. Record and compare the height of your four muffins in the table below.

SAFETY ALERT!

Be sure to wear oven mitts when removing the muffins from the microwave oven.

Muffin Height Data Chart

Batch	Baking soda	Cream of tartar	Height
1	no	yes	
2	yes	no	
3	yes	yes	
4	no	no	

Analyze the Results

11. Compare your results with your prediction, and explain any differences.

_____

_____

_____

_____

_____

_____

PHYSICAL SCIENCE

Fiber-Optic Fun

Purpose
This teacher demonstration shows how fiber optics allows communication by total internal reflection through a material.

Time Required
One 45-minute class period

Lab Ratings
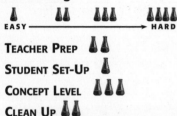

EASY —————————→ HARD

TEACHER PREP

STUDENT SET-UP

CONCEPT LEVEL

CLEAN UP

MATERIALS

- 1 envelope unflavored gelatin
- 250 mL of hot water
- miniature loaf pan or shallow plastic-foam tray
- refrigerator
- laser pointer or index card and slide projector
- metric ruler
- utility knife or razor blade

Advance Preparation
Make double-strength gelatin by dissolving one envelope (7 g) of unflavored gelatin mix in 250 mL of hot water. Pour the gelatin into a miniature loaf pan. A rectangular, shallow plastic-foam tray similar to those used in meat or fruit packaging will also work well. Chill the gelatin in a refrigerator for at least 1 hour. Leave the gelatin in the refrigerator until immediately before the demonstration.

You can order an inexpensive laser pointer from a laboratory materials supplier, such as Science Kit (800-828-7777; approximately $20). A laser pointer works best, but if one is not available, use a slide projector. However, you will need to narrow the beam. To do so, use an index card

to make a paper square the size of a photographic slide. Then punch a small hole in the center of the card. Put the card in the projector so that light exits only through the hole. The slide-projector beam will be easier to see if you clap chalkboard erasers into the air between the projector and the gelatin. Dimming the room lights will also help.

You may wish to practice this demonstration before performing it for the class. Review the concepts of reflection and refraction with students before performing the activity. As students answer the questions during the demonstration, they may find it helpful to draw what they see.

You may also wish to make flavored gelatin for students to eat after completing the activity.

Instructions for completing the demonstration follow. Also provided is a corresponding student worksheet, pages 116–117.

Safety Information
Make sure that the laser is never pointed directly at a person's face. This can lead to serious eye injury.

In-Class Demonstration
1. It is important for students to have an unobstructed view of the gelatin mold. If the sides of the plastic-foam tray or loaf pan prevent students from viewing the demonstration from the side, transfer the gelatin mold onto a sheet of cardboard.

2. Use a utility knife or a razor blade to cut the gelatin into strips approximately 2.5 cm wide. The cuts should be made parallel to the long sides of the gelatin mold. The strips represent fiber-optic cables.

continued...

Tracy Jahn
Berkshire Junior High
Canaan, New York

3. Choose one of the strips as your fiber-optic cable. Shine the light from one end of the strip into the gelatin at an incident angle of 0° (perpendicular to the surface of the gelatin). Note that the incident angle is measured from the beam to an imaginary line perpendicular to the surface. Ask students to note how the path and brightness of the light beam varies as the beam travels through the gelatin.

4. Have students answer question 1 on their worksheet.

5. Slightly increase the incident angle of the light beam, and have students observe the difference between the brightness of the refracted ray and the brightness of the reflected ray. Then have students answer question 2.

6. Ask students to make a prediction about how the brightness will change as you continue to increase the incidence angle of the light beam. Then have students answer question 3.

7. Ask students to predict whether the behavior they described in question 3 will continue for all incident angles. What do they think will ultimately happen to the beam? Then have students answer question 4.

8. Continue increasing the incident angle, bringing the beam more parallel to the surface, until you reach the critical angle. For water, the critical angle is 49°. At this angle, no light will be refracted out of the sides of the gelatin strip. Instead, the light will exhibit total internal reflection.

9. Discuss the process of total internal reflection with students. Then have students apply their knowledge to telephone lines by answering question 5 on their worksheet.

Discussion

When a beam of light hits the interface between two transparent materials, such as air and gelatin, part of the beam is reflected and part of the beam is transmitted through the interface. The transmitted beam is usually bent, or refracted, as it passes into the different material.

The farther the beam is from the perpendicular (the larger the incident angle when the beam hits the surface), the more the beam is refracted. If the light is moving from a more dense material into a less dense material (for example, from gelatin into air), the light bends toward the surface. At the critical angle, the bending, or refraction, will be so strong that the refracted beam will be directed along the surface; that is, none of the beam will be transmitted into the air.

When the incident angle is larger than the critical angle, all the light is reflected back into the gelatin; therefore, the reflected beam is nearly as bright as the incident beam. This phenomenon is called total internal reflection because nearly 100 percent of the beam is reflected.

Evaluation Strategies

For help evaluating this lab, see the Self Evaluation of Learning Skills in the *Assessment Checklists & Rubrics*.

This checklist is also available in the *One-Stop Planner CD-ROM*.

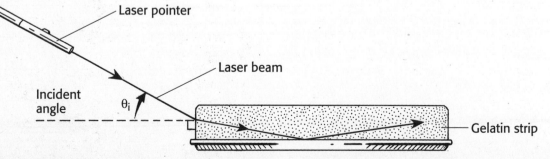

Laser pointer

Laser beam

Incident angle

θ_i

Gelatin strip

PHYSICAL SCIENCE

MAKING MODELS

Fiber-Optic Fun

Have you ever seen telephone workers installing new telephone cables along the highway? The cables are probably not made of copper wire, which carries electrical energy, but of fine, glass fibers that carry light. As amazing as it seems, long-distance telephone companies transmit conversations in the form of tiny pulses of light.

Telephone companies make use of the process of *total internal reflection* to keep a signal from weakening too rapidly over long distances or from leaking out of the fiber as the signal bounces around in the fiber.

When total internal reflection occurs, the pulses of light traveling along an optical fiber act like stones skipping across the surface of a quiet pond. But instead of eventually falling down into the water the way a stone does, the light is reflected into the air.

In this activity, your teacher will demonstrate how fiber optics are used to transmit telephone conversations. Follow along by answering the questions below.

Ask a Question

How does total internal reflection allow fiber optics to transmit telephone conversations?

Collect Data

1. Describe the path of the beam of light.

   _____

   _____

   _____

2. Describe the path and the brightness of the beam after your teacher has moved it slightly.

   _____

   _____

   _____

   _____

Make a Prediction

3. What do you think will happen if your teacher continues to move the beam in the same direction?

_____

_____

_____

4. Based on your answer to number 3, what do you think will ultimately happen to the beam?

_____

_____

_____

Draw Conclusions

5. How does total internal reflection allow fiber optics to transmit telephone conversations?

_____

_____

_____

_____

Going Further

Investigate the structure of fiber-optic cables in greater detail. Questions you may wish to consider include the following:
- What are fiber-optic cables made of?
- How many signals can a fiber-optic cable transmit at one time?
- What is transmitted in a fiber-optic cable? How does this differ from a metal cable?
- In what ways are fiber-optic cables an improvement over metal cables?

PHYSICAL SCIENCE

Art Credits

All art, unless otherwise noted, by Holt, Rinehart and Winston.

Abbreviated as follows: (t) top; (b) bottom; (c) center; (r) right; (l) left; (bkgd) background. Front cover (owl), Kim Taylor/Bruce Coleman, Inc.; Page 8 (cl), Elizabeth Morales; 18 (tr), Carlyn Iverson; 22 (tr), Len Shalansky; 25 (t), Len Shalansky; 28 (tr), David Merrell; 30 (bc), Laurie O'Keefe; 33 (b), Carlyn Iverson; 35 (tl), Carlyn Iverson; 38 (tr), David Merrell; 42 (tr), Carlyn Iverson; 47 (tr), David Merrell; 51 (tr), Len Shalansky; 56 (tr), Guy Wolek; 59 (c), Guy Wolek; 62 (b), David Merrell; 65 (bc), Elizabeth Morales; 67 (tr) Precision Graphics; 72 (tr) Elizabeth Morales; 73 (tl), Elizabeth Morales; 73 (cl), Elizabeth Morales; 73 (bl), Elizabeth Morales; 77 (tr), Carlyn Iverson; 82 (tr), Carlyn Iverson; 92 (tr), David Merrell; 96 (tr), Len Shalansky; 96 (b), Precision Graphics; 105 (tr), David Merrell; 108 (tr), Laurie O'Keefe; 111 (tr), Guy Wolek; 115 (b), Carlyn Iverson; 116 (tr), David Merrell

Answer Key

Labs You Can Eat

▪ CONTENTS ▪

Say Cheese! continued

pH Test Results

	Milk	Lemon juice	Whey
pH	6.7	3.0	4.8

5. Was the pH of the whey the same as that of plain milk? Why or why not?

   No. The added lemon juice made the whey more acidic.

6. Line the sieve or strainer with three layers of cheesecloth, and place it in a sink. Pour the contents of the saucepan into the sieve or strainer.

7. Allow the curd to drain for 1 minute. You now have cottage cheese!

8. Do you think the whey contains the same amount of protein as plain milk contains? Why or why not?

   No. The protein in the milk turned to curd, so there is less protein in the whey.

Near Paneer?

Now follow steps 9–12 to make *paneer*, a popular cheese in India.

9. Gather the edges of the cheesecloth and twist them over the sink, pressing out as much whey as possible.

10. Use the piece of twine to tie off the cheesecloth bag. Suspend the bag over a sink or bucket so that it will drain overnight.

11. In the morning, untie and loosen the bundle. Keeping the cheesecloth wrapped around the cheese, flatten the cheese slightly on top of the plate. Place the water-filled pot or other heavy object on top of the cheese for 4–5 hours.

12. At the end of this time, the cheese should be compressed to a thickness of 1.5–2 cm. Remove the weight and the cheesecloth. You now have paneer! The cheese is ready to be cut into cubes.

The Incredible Edible Cell, continued

Name _____ Date _____ Class _____

Analysis

14. How were the structures in the cell your group created similar to the structures in the cell you received from the other group?

Sample answer: Both cells contained an endoplasmic reticulum, a

Golgi complex, ribosomes, a cell membrane, mitochondria, and a

nucleus.

15. How did the cell structures differ?

Sample answer: Our cell was a plant cell, but the other group's cell

was an animal cell. Our cell contained chloroplasts, vacuoles, and a

cell wall, but theirs did not. Their cell contained lysosomes and cen-

trioles, but ours did not.

Critical Thinking

16. Explain any differences in the contents of a plant cell and an animal cell in terms of the function of the cell.

Animal cells don't contain chloroplasts because they don't make

their own food through photosynthesis. Animal cells don't contain

vacuoles because they don't need a location to store water and

keep their shape the way plants do. Animal cells don't have cell

walls because they have to be able to move. Plant cells do not need

lysosomes to function. Instead, plants use their vacuoles as giant

lysosomes.

Answer to Going Further:
Encourage students to be creative when developing their blueprints. Nerve cells and red blood cells exhibit structural features that are different from the animal and plant cells modeled in this activity. For example, nerve cells have dendrites and axons while red blood cells lack a nucleus or mitochondria. The human body is made up of over 100 different types of cells.

Going Further

Research a specialized cell, such as a nerve cell or a red blood cell. Then develop a blueprint for an edible model of that cell using edible items. In doing so, consider how the structures in the specialized cell differ from the structures in a typical animal or plant cell.

Say Cheese! continued

Name _____ Date _____ Class _____

Are You a Cheese Whiz?

Critical Thinking

13. In this activity, you studied how changing the acidity of a protein's environment changed the solubility of the protein. This caused the protein to behave differently.

As another example of the importance of the environment on protein function, consider blood. Blood contains large quantities of dissolved proteins. Use your experience from this lab to predict what might happen to these proteins if blood pH suddenly dropped significantly.

The protein in blood serum might become insoluble and "curdle"

like milk protein.

What might be a danger of such a drop in pH for circulatory function?

The insoluble protein could block veins and arteries.

Answer to Going Further:
The linear sequence of amino acids in a protein is the protein's primary structure. Interactions between the amino acids cause the linear protein to bend into a new shape, such as a helix. This new shape is the secondary structure of a protein. The structure that results from the interactions of large segments of the protein is the tertiary structure. Finally, some proteins are made of two or more amino acid chains, which can be the same or different. The combined structure is the quaternary structures.

Going Further

As milk curdles, the shape of the protein molecules in the milk changes, causing the protein to become insoluble. But what does it mean for a protein to change shape? Research the primary, secondary, tertiary, and quaternary structure of a protein molecule. Then write a short paragraph explaining what these structures are. Some changes to these structures will affect the function of the protein molecule.

4   HOLT SCIENCE AND TECHNOLOGY

Name _____ Date _____ Class _____

The Mystery of the Runny Gelatin, continued

12. What might the meat tenderizer have in common with the fruit(s) that kept the gelatin from setting?

The meat tenderizer, figs, pineapple, papaya, and kiwi all might contain papain or a similar enzyme that splits protein and keeps the gelatin from setting.

13. How did Uva's preparation differ this time from previous times?

All of the fruits she used were fresh this time. Previously, Uva used canned fruits in addition to the fresh fruits.

14. Based on what you have learned in this activity, what do you think happens to fresh fruit in the canning process? How would this affect the enzymes in the fruit?

Canned fruit is heated. The heating process destroys enzymes.

Critical Thinking

15. Use what you have learned from this activity to help Uva revise her recipe.

Boil the papaya, figs, kiwi, and pineapple long enough to deactivate their protein-splitting enzymes before adding them to the salad.

Name _____ Date _____ Class _____

The Mystery of the Runny Gelatin, continued

Day 2: The Plot Thickens

8. On the next day, remove the tray from the refrigerator. Place a bowl or dish under each sample. Gently tip each cup to see whether the contents are soft and runny or are gelled and firm. If the mixture has gelled, write *yes* in the Gel Set column of the Data Table. If some of the contents begins to drip, write *no* in the Gel Set column.

9. Clean up as directed by your teacher.

10. Review the evidence and clues you've gathered in the Data Table and from Hugo's note pad. Then help Detective Naranja answer Ms. Plantana's questions.

NOTE PAD: From the desk of

H. Naranja

Important clues:

Enzyme—a protein that speeds up certain chemical reactions. Enzymes have a variety of functions, including breaking down other proteins

Bromelain—a protein-splitting enzyme in some fruit

Gelatin—a protein that forms a soft gel when mixed with warm liquid and that forms a firm gel when the liquid is cooled. Damaging this protein will prevent gel formation

Papain—a protein-splitting enzyme found in fruit; a common ingredient of some meat tenderizers

Hugo's Advice

11. Did the gelatin fail to set in any of the cups? If so, list the contents of those cups.

Answers will vary, depending on labeling and the types of fruit used.

Sample answer: Yes, the gelatin failed to set in the cups containing the meat tenderizer (#2) and the samples of fig, kiwi, papaya, and pineapple.

Name _____ Date _____ Class _____

SKILL BUILDER

Bacterial Buddies

Many people think of bacteria as nasty and life-threatening, even though not all bacteria are harmful. In fact, some bacteria actually help us. Believe it or not, people add bacteria to food to help preserve it!

Milk will spoil quickly if it is not refrigerated. Ancient cultures found a way to preserve milk without refrigeration. They used certain types of bacteria to ferment the milk and turn it into yogurt. These bacteria feed on sugar in the milk, producing lactic acid in the process. The acid helps to prevent the growth of other, harmful bacteria and gives yogurt its sour taste.

In this lab, you will observe the fermentation of milk and the resulting change in acidity as milk turns into yogurt.

Ask a Question

1. How do some bacteria help to preserve milk by turning it into yogurt?

Conduct an Experiment

2. While wearing the oven mitts, heat the milk in the saucepan to a temperature of 80°C. Do not allow the milk to boil. Maintain the milk at 80°C for 5 minutes while stirring continuously. Remove the saucepan from heat. **Caution:** Be careful when working around the hot stove.

3. Let the milk cool to about 44°C.

4. Use the pH paper to measure the acidity of the milk in the saucepan.
Starting pH of milk in the saucepan _____ 7

5. Pour 150 mL of the warm milk into the beaker labeled "No culture."

6. Measure the pH of the live-culture yogurt.
pH of premade, live-culture yogurt _____ 4

7. Stir 20 mL of yogurt into the milk that remains in the saucepan, (150 mL) and mix well. Measure the pH.
Starting pH of milk and yogurt mixture _____ 6

MATERIALS
- 300 mL of nonfat milk
- large saucepan
- cooking thermometer
- watch or clock
- oven mitts
- hot plate
- pH paper and color scale
- 100 mL graduated cylinder
- 200 mL beakers (2), one labeled "No culture" and the other "Culture"
- waterproof marker for labeling
- live yogurt culture
- stirring spoon
- dish towel

Name _____ Date _____ Class _____

The Mystery of the Runny Gelatin, continued

Gel Set Data Table

Sample	Contents	Prediction: Will the gel set?	Actual: Did the gel set?
1	liquid gelatin		
2	liquid gelatin with meat tenderizer		
3	Information in this data chart will vary, depending on samples used.		
4	Data should be clear and precise.		
5			
6			
7			
8			
9			

Answer to Going Further:
These enzymes help to break down (digest) the proteins in the stomach.

Going Further

Some people take tablets that contain enzymes from papaya and pineapple to counter the effects of indigestion. How do these tablets work?

Name _____ Date _____ Class _____

Bacterial Buddies, continued

12. Why was it important to have a beaker in which no live culture was introduced?

This beaker was the control. It showed what happens to milk when

it's not mixed with yogurt bacteria.

13. Which beaker showed the greatest change in pH? Why do you think that happened?

The beaker with the added culture showed the greatest change in

pH. This was because the added bacteria produced acid.

Draw Conclusions

14. Based on the results of this activity, how do you think the addition of live-culture yogurt helps to keep milk from spoiling?

The bacteria in the live culture produce acid, which prevents bad

bacteria from growing and spoiling the milk.

Answer to Going Further:

Two examples of helpful bacteria are some strains of *E. coli* and *Rhizobium*. Helpful *E. coli* live in the digestive tracts of all vertebrates, including humans, and provide us with vitamin K, which is necessary for blood to clot. *Rhizobium* are nitrogen-fixing bacteria that usually live in nodules on the roots of legumes. They enable legumes to grow in nitrogen-poor soils.

Going Further

Are there other kinds of friendly bacteria besides those in yogurt? What are they, and how do they help living organisms?

Name _____ Date _____ Class _____

▶▶▶ **LIFE SCIENCE**

Bacterial Buddies, continued

8. Pour the mixture into the beaker labeled "Culture."

9. Place both beakers in a place designated by your teacher, and then cover them with a dish towel.

10. After 24 hours, retrieve the beakers and evaluate the contents of each for pH, smell, and appearance. Record the results in the Yogurt Log on this page.

Yogurt Log

Beaker	Appearance	Smell	pH
No culture	Slightly thickened; no color change	Smells spoiled	6
Culture	Color is mostly white; texture is firm and thick; a clear fluid has separated from the milk	Smells slightly acidic or "yogurty"	4

Analyze the Results

11. How did the contents of the beakers differ in smell and appearance on the second day?

The sample in the beaker labeled "No culture" is liquid and has a

bad smell. The beaker labeled "Culture" contains a thick, white sub-

stance that smells and appears similar to the yogurt that was added

to the milk yesterday.

Name _____ Date _____ Class _____

Knot Your Average Yeast Lab, continued

Beaker Observations

Beaker 1: warm water and yeast
The mixture is slightly cloudy, but nothing is happening.

Beaker 2: warm water, yeast, and sugar
Little bubbles keep moving to the surface and bursting. Lots of bubbles are forming. It seems active. The bubbles are probably carbon dioxide.

Beaker 3: hot water and yeast
The mixture is slightly cloudy, but nothing is happening.

Beaker 4: hot water, yeast, and sugar
The mixture is slightly cloudy, but nothing is happening.

6. Is sugar necessary for the yeast to produce carbon dioxide? Explain.

Yes. Only the yeast with warm water and sugar produced carbon

dioxide bubbles. The yeast in water alone did not cause any change.

7. Select the beaker that is best-suited for making pretzels. Explain your choice.

Beaker 2 is the best choice because it is the only beaker in which

bubbles are forming. The bubbles show that the yeast is active.

Name _____ Date _____ Class _____

Knot Your Average Yeast Lab

SKILL BUILDER

Have you ever wondered what makes dough rise? Believe it or not, dough rises because of a fungus—a tiny, living, one-celled organism called *yeast*. When dried, yeast are in a state of suspended animation. But when you add warm water and sugar, watch out! The yeast get active and go into a feeding frenzy. What's left behind is carbon dioxide and alcohol.

In this activity, you can watch yeast at work!

MATERIALS

- 500 mL beakers (4) or jars
- waterproof marker for labeling
- 2 packages of active dry yeast
- 750 mL of warm water about 40°C
- 750 mL of hot water, approx 80°C
- 16 mL (3 tsp) of sugar
- thermometer
- 4 stirring spoons
- watch or clock
- mixing bowl
- 650 mL of all-purpose flour
- 8 mL (1½ tsp) of salt
- mixing spoon
- roll of plastic wrap
- refrigerator
- paper plates
- microwave
- paper towels

Objective

To observe the effects of yeast activity on pretzel dough

Day 1: Activate Those Yeast Cells!

1. Label the beakers 1–4. Add one-half package of yeast to each beaker.

2. Add ingredients to each beaker according to the following directions:

Beaker 1: 325 mL warm water
Beaker 2: 325 mL warm water and 8 mL sugar
Beaker 3: 325 mL hot water
Beaker 4: 325 mL hot water and 8 mL sugar

3. Using a separate stirring rod each time, gently stir the contents of each beaker. Wait three minutes.

4. Observe the contents of each beaker for a few seconds. What is happening in the beakers? Record and explain your observations in the chart on page 23.

5. What do your lab results tell you about the effect temperature has on the carbon–dioxide production of yeast?

Yeast seems to do well in warm water and poorly in hot water. The

yeast didn't do anything in the beakers with hot water, but they were

very active in one of the warm-water beakers—the one containing

sugar.

Name _____ Date _____ Class _____

Knot Your Average Yeast Lab, continued

8. Pour the contents of the beaker you select into the mixing bowl. Make sure that all of the mixture is transferred to the bowl.

9. Add 125 mL of flour and 8 mL of salt to the yeast mixture, and mix well. Slowly add more flour until dough begins to form. You will add approximately 500 mL of flour. The remaining flour will be used to flour the kneading surface.

10. Sprinkle a handful of flour evenly on a large, flat surface. Turn the dough onto the floured surface, and begin to knead it. Knead by repeatedly pushing the palms of your hands into the dough. Every few seconds, turn the dough a quarter turn, and fold the dough over. You will need to add more flour to the surface of the dough and the table as the dough gets sticky. Continue kneading for about five minutes. Stop kneading when the dough no longer feels sticky and is smooth and elastic.

11. Place the dough back in the bowl. Cover the bowl with plastic wrap, and label it for your group. Refrigerate the dough overnight.

Day 2: Let's All Do the Twist!

12. Remove the dough from the refrigerator. What differences do you notice in the dough's appearance? Record your observations.

The dough seems to have doubled in size. It appears to be spongier

and full of air pockets.

_____

_____

13. Using your observations from the day before, explain why the dough's appearance has changed.

The dough's appearance has changed because the yeast continued

to produce carbon dioxide. The carbon dioxide formed air pockets

in the dough.

_____

Name _____ Date _____ Class _____

Knot Your Average Yeast Lab, continued

14. Pull off a piece of dough the size of a golf ball, and roll it into a long, snakelike shape. Fold the dough into a pretzel shape using the diagrams below as your guide.

15. Place the unbaked pretzels on paper plates. Cook them in the microwave at low to medium (30%) power for 2–3 minutes. Your pretzels are ready when they are dry and slightly springy to the touch.

HELPFUL HINT

The pretzels will not turn brown in a microwave oven—do not overbake them.

16. Carefully remove the pretzels from the oven, and allow them to cool for five minutes.

17. Break a piece off the end of the pretzel, and look inside.

What Happened?

18. What does the inside of the pretzel look like?

It is the color of the dough and contains many small holes.

_____

19. What caused the inside of the pretzel to look like it does?

The carbon dioxide trapped in the dough created air pockets.

_____

Name _____ Date _____ Class _____

Not Just Another Nut

You might be surprised to hear that peanuts aren't nuts at all. Also known as goobers, groundnuts, or earthnuts, peanuts are legumes. Legumes are the fruit of a particular type of plant. Unlike most legumes, peanuts ripen underground instead of aboveground. In the southern United States, the tops of peanut plants are used to feed livestock.

In this activity, you will look at the peanut seed and peanut sprout in greater detail.

MATERIALS

- paper plate
- raw, unshelled peanut seed pod, soaked overnight
- toothpick
- magnifying glass
- cup containing peanut sprout

USEFUL TERMS

seed coat
reddish, paper-thin covering around each peanut seed

hilum
a scar on the seed indicating where the seed was attached to the fruit

cotyledons
nutrient-heavy, fleshy halves of the legume seed

embryonic leaves
tiny leaves inside the seed

embryonic root
rootlike part inside the seed

SCIENTIFIC METHOD

Make a Prediction

1. What is the function of a peanut seed in the growth of a peanut plant?

Sample answer: The peanut seed supplies the growing plant with

food and protection. _____

_____

Make Observations

2. On the paper plate, carefully open the peanut seed pod to retrieve the seeds inside. Gently open one of the seeds by sliding the two halves past each other. Use the toothpick if needed.

3. Examine each half of the seed with the magnifying glass. Use the Useful Terms at left to identify as many structures as you can.

Collect Data

4. Sketch both halves of the peanut seed in the space provided on page 30. Label the following parts: embryonic leaves, embryonic root, cotyledons, hilum, and seed coat.

Name _____ Date _____ Class _____

Knot Your Average Yeast Lab, continued

20. Do you notice any evidence of the alcohol that the yeast produced? Explain your answer.

No. The alcohol must have evaporated while the dough cooked.

_____

_____

_____

_____

21. If you had used the contents of a different beaker to make the dough, how might the pretzels have been different?

The pretzels would not have had the pockets of carbon dioxide in

them, and therefore, the dough would not have risen.

_____

_____

_____

Critical Thinking

22. The heat from the oven killed the yeast and no more carbon dioxide was produced. So why did the dough continue to rise during the baking process?

Gas expands when it is heated; the gas that was already in the

dough began to expand once it was heated.

_____

Name _____ Date _____ Class _____

Not Just Another Nut, continued

USEFUL TERMS

primary root root of the sprout

shoot stem and leaves of the sprout

5. Remove the peanut sprout from the cup, and carefully examine the plant. Sketch the sprout in the space provided on page 30. Use the Useful Terms to identify and label the parts.

Analyze the Results

6. Compare your sketches for the peanut seed and the sprouted peanut. What structures have changed as the plant has grown?

The cotyledons are shriveling up. The seed coat has fallen off. The seed has grown into a peanut sprout, and the embryonic root is now a primary root.

Draw Conclusions

7. What do you think is the purpose of the hard shell that you removed from the peanut at the beginning of the lab? (Hint: Think about where the fruit of the peanut plant grows.)

Sample answer: The hard shell protects the fruit as it ripens underground.

8. How would you explain the change in the appearance of the cotyledons in the sprout?

As the sprout grew, it used the nutrients in the cotyledons, causing the cotyledons to shrivel.

Answer to Going Further:
George Washington Carver realized that cotton crops tended to deplete the soil of nutrients. Growing legumes, such as peanuts, however, helped restore the soil with needed protein and nitrogen. Some of the products he developed from peanuts included cheese, flour, ink, plastics, wood stains, soap, and cosmetics.

Going Further

George Washington Carver was a scientist who urged farmers in the southern United States to plant peanuts. He is known for researching and developing more than 300 products from peanuts. Find out why he encouraged farmers to grow peanuts, and list at least five products that he derived from peanuts.

Name _____ Date _____ Class _____

Not Just Another Nut, continued

Legume Observations

Peanut (seed)

Student drawings will vary but should clearly identify all of the structures listed in the Useful Terms on page 28.

Peanut (sprout)

Student drawings will vary but should clearly identify most if not all of the following features: shriveled cotyledons, primary shoot, and primary root.

Name _____ Date _____ Class _____

Here's Looking at You, Squid! continued

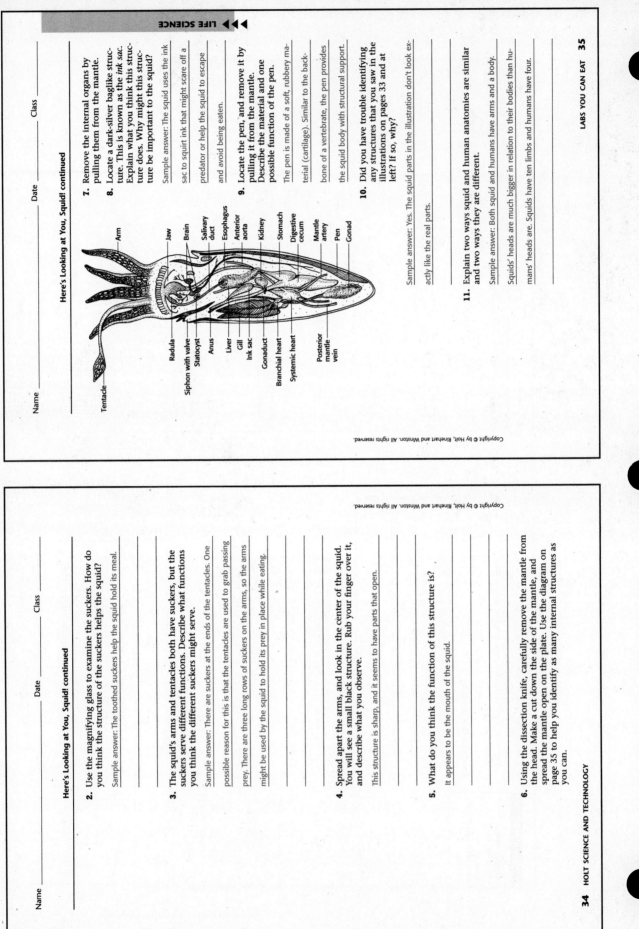

7. Remove the internal organs by pulling them from the mantle.

8. Locate a dark-silver baglike structure. This is known as the *ink sac*. Explain what you think this structure does. Why might this structure be important to the squid?

Sample answer: The squid uses the ink sac to squirt ink that might scare off a predator or help the squid to escape and avoid being eaten.

9. Locate the pen, and remove it by pulling it from the mantle. Describe the material and one possible function of the pen.

The pen is made of a soft, rubbery material (cartilage). Similar to the backbone of a vertebrate, the pen provides the squid body with structural support.

10. Did you have trouble identifying any structures that you saw in the illustrations on pages 33 and at left? If so, why?

Sample answer: Yes. The squid parts in the illustration don't look exactly like the real parts.

_____

11. Explain two ways squid and human anatomies are similar and two ways they are different.

Sample answer: Both squid and humans have arms and a body.

Squids' heads are much bigger in relation to their bodies than humans' heads are. Squids have ten limbs and humans have four.

Name _____ Date _____ Class _____

Here's Looking at You, Squid! continued

2. Use the magnifying glass to examine the suckers. How do you think the structure of the suckers helps the squid?

Sample answer: The toothed suckers help the squid hold its meal.

_____

3. The squid's arms and tentacles both have suckers, but the suckers serve different functions. Describe what functions you think the different suckers might serve.

Sample answer: There are suckers at the ends of the tentacles. One possible reason for this is that the tentacles are used to grab passing prey. There are three long rows of suckers on the arms, so the arms might be used by the squid to hold its prey in place while eating.

_____

4. Spread apart the arms, and look in the center of the squid. You will see a small black structure. Rub your finger over it, and describe what you observe.

This structure is sharp, and it seems to have parts that open.

_____

5. What do you think the function of this structure is?

It appears to be the mouth of the squid.

_____

6. Using the dissection knife, carefully remove the mantle from the head. Make a cut down the side of the mantle, and spread the mantle open on the plate. Use the diagram on page 35 to help you identify as many internal structures as you can.

Name _____ Date _____ Class _____

Why Birds of a Beak Eat Together, continued

8. How does your answer compare with your prediction at the beginning of this activity?

Answers will vary, depending on students' original predictions.
Students may find that their beak model works well in more than one habitat. However, encourage students to decide in which habitat their beak works best.

9. Based on the results of this activity, why do you think beaks have adapted the way they have?

Birds have evolved specialized beaks in response to the unique conditions of their environment.

Critical Thinking

10. What would happen if the habitat to which your flock were best suited were destroyed? Are there any other habitats in which your flock could easily survive? Justify your answer.

Sample answer: The hawk uses a forklike beak to spear its food.
This beak could also be used to pick up small insects from bark.

Answer to Going Further:
In the class discussion, be sure that students relate what they learned in the video to what they learned in this activity.

Going Further

Watch a video about the eating habits of birds that live in different habitats. Then discuss with the rest of the class what you learned from the video.

Name _____ Date _____ Class _____

Why Birds of a Beak Eat Together, continued

Feeding Chart

Habitat	Feeding results
1	Answers will vary, depending on circumstances. However, students should describe their feeding results with clear and precise details.
2	
3	
4	
5	
6	
7	

Beak-ause All Birds Are Different

7. In which habitat was it easiest for your flock to obtain food? Explain.

Answers will vary, depending on specific materials and equipment, but students should provide clear and logical explanations for their answer.

► ► **LIFE SCIENCE**

Name _____ Date _____ Class _____

A Salty Sweet Experiment, continued

Analyze the Results

9. According to your results, which areas of the tongue were most sensitive to the following tastes?

Sour: ____C____

Sweet: ____A____

Bitter: ____D____

Salty: ____B____

10. Which regions of the tongue, if any, detected only one taste sensation?

Region D detected only bitter taste.

Draw Conclusions

11. Tondy was unable to taste the sweetness of the ice cream. Give one explanation for this.

Sample answer: When Tondy burned her tongue, she may have

damaged the taste buds that are most sensitive to sweet things, so

it was hard to taste sweetness.

12. Why might the ice cream have tasted salty to Tondy?

Sample answer: The ice cream probably came into contact with

Tondy's salty taste buds. The ice cream tasted salty instead of sweet

because her sweet taste buds were damaged.

Name _____ Date _____ Class _____

A Salty Sweet Experiment, continued

LIFE SCIENCE ◄◄

Taste Response

Region of the tongue	Sample type	Strength of taste (first taster)	Strength of taste (second taster)
A	Sour	weak	no taste
	Sweet	strong	strong
	Salty	weak	weak
	Bitter	no taste	no taste
B	Sour	strong	strong
	Sweet	no taste	no taste
	Salty	weak	weak
	Bitter	no taste	no taste
C	Sour	weak	weak
	Sweet	no taste	no taste
	Salty	strong	strong
	Bitter	no taste	no taste
D	Sour	no taste	no taste
	Sweet	no taste	no taste
	Salty	no taste	no taste
	Bitter	strong	strong

Worksheet 1 (Snack Attack)

Name _____ Date _____ Class _____

LAB 10 — STUDENT WORKSHEET

SKILL BUILDER

Snack Attack

Elizabeth Goose is throwing the party of the year, but health-conscious Jack Spratt eats only foods that are low in fat. Liz gave him a list of foods she is planning to serve at the party, but Jack is worried—he doesn't know how to tell the fatty foods from the low-fat foods. Can you help him figure out what foods he should eat at the party?

MATERIALS
- large brown paper bag
- scissors
- metric ruler
- 6 samples of various snack foods
- avocado
- apple
- nutritional labels from the various snack foods used
- paper towels

Objective

To determine the relative amount of fat in a variety of snack foods

Day 1: Getting Ready

1. Cut the front and rear panels from a paper bag.

2. Draw a grid with 3 columns and 3 rows on the panel of brown paper. Each square in the grid should be about 10 × 10 cm.

3. You will be testing eight food samples. Place one sample in the center of a square on the grid. Label the square for that sample.

4. Repeat step 3 for each of the other samples.

5. Label the test panel with your group information, and set it in a place where it will be undisturbed for 24 hours.

Day 2: Finding That Sneaky Fat

6. Retrieve your test panel, and carefully remove and discard the food from the paper.

7. Observe any differences in the paper in each square. Can you tell where the fat was absorbed by the paper? Explain.

Yes. At the places where the fat was absorbed, the paper is easier to

see through when held up to the light.

Worksheet 2 (A Salty Sweet Experiment, continued)

Name _____ Date _____ Class _____

A Salty Sweet Experiment, continued

13. Most deadly poisons are extremely bitter. What would be the advantage of having the back part of the tongue detect only bitter tastes?

Detecting bitter substances at the back of the tongue might stimu-

late the gagging reflex that would help to eliminate the substance

before swallowing it.

Answer to Going Further:

Because of genetic differences, some people find amaranth to be extremely bitter while others find it to be nutty.

Going Further

Foods do not always taste the same to different people. Amaranth, a grain, is one such food. Research amaranth to learn more about what it tastes like to different people and what causes this variation.

Name _____ Date _____ Class _____

Snack Attack, continued

What Should Jack Eat?

11. Which food left the stain with the largest diameter?

Sample answer: The potato chips made the largest fat stain.

12. Which food contained the highest percentage of fat?

Sample answer: The potato chips contained the highest percentage of fat.

13. Which two foods should Jack eat to avoid fat?

Sample answer: Jack should eat the baked potato chips and the apple because they have no fat.

14. Which two foods should Jack avoid? Explain your answer.

Sample answer: Jack should avoid the candy bar and the avocado because they have the highest percentage of fat.

Critical Thinking

15. You may have noticed when testing the apple sample that a large circle appeared and then disappeared. What do you think happened?

Water from the apple soaked into the paper and then evaporated.

Going Further

Some fats are healthier than others. Fats may be monounsaturated, polyunsaturated, or saturated. Avocados are very high in monounsaturated fat. Find out why the type of fat you eat may be just as important as the amount of fat you eat.

Answer to Going Further:

Fat is stored energy, and it helps our bodies absorb some vitamins. However, too much fat can lead to heart disease and other health problems. *Monounsaturated fat* is found in most vegetable oils and is usually a liquid at room temperature, although it congeals in the refrigerator. *Polyunsaturated fat* is commonly found in vegetables and in nuts like sesame, sunflower, safflower, and walnut. This type of fat is usually liquid at room temperature, but it doesn't congeal in the refrigerator. *Saturated fats* are found in most animal products and some tropical oils and are solid at room temperature. They are closely linked to heart disease.

Name _____ Date _____ Class _____

Snack Attack, continued

8. Measure the diameter of the circles that remain on the paper. In ascending order of size, record the substances and measurements in the Fat-Content Results Table below.

Fat-Content Results Table

Food sample	Diameter of fat stain (cm)	Percentage of fat

9. Read the nutritional label for each packaged snack and record the percentages of total fat for each snack on the chart. What is the relationship between the diameter of the fat stain and the percentage of fat for the packaged foods?

The greater the percentage of fat in the food, the larger the fat stain.

10. Compare the size of the fat stains for the avocado and the apple with the size of the fat stains for the other foods. Use those comparisons to estimate the percentage of fat for the avocado and the apple. Record your answers in the chart.

Copyright © by Holt, Rinehart and Winston. All rights reserved.

Name _____ Date _____ Class _____

LAB 11 STUDENT WORKSHEET

MAKING MODELS

Famous Rock Groups

When is a rock a liquid? When it melts, of course! But melting is just one part of the rock cycle.

A rock can follow many paths in the rock cycle. For example, a molten rock cools and hardens to form igneous rock. Mechanical weathering or erosion can later break the rock down into tiny particles. These particles build up in layers to form sedimentary rock. As the layers accumulate, their weight adds pressure to lower layers, and the combined heat and pressure can compress the rock below to create metamorphic rock. When the temperature and pressure become great enough, the metamorphic rock melts. The cycle can then continue on the same pathway or a completely different pathway.

In this activity, you will get a chance to make a tasty model of one pathway through the rock cycle.

MATERIALS
- sheet of waxed paper
- 4 types of candy chips, 50 mL each
- metric ruler
- 4 sharp knives or scissors
- heavy aluminum foil, 25 × 25 cm
- 2 large, heavy books (such as dictionaries or large textbooks)
- aluminum pie plate, 20 cm in diameter or larger
- hot plate
- 2 oven mitts

◄◄ ►► EARTH SCIENCE

Objective
To simulate the formation of sedimentary, metamorphic, and igneous rock

A Chip Off the Old Rock

1. Cover your work area with a sheet of wax paper, and place one of the types of chips on it. Shave the chips into small pieces with a knife or scissors. **Caution:** Be careful not to cut yourself!

2. Repeat step 1 for the other chips, making sure to keep the shavings in separate piles.

3. In your model of the rock cycle, what do the following items represent?

- The whole chips: The whole chips represent rocks.

- The knife or scissors: The knife represents forces of mechanical weathering.

- The chip shavings: The shavings represent sediment, or particles worn away by weathering.

4. Fold the sheet of aluminum foil in half. Place the foil on your workspace, and open it up so that the crease is in the middle.

LABS YOU CAN EAT 51

Copyright © by Holt, Rinehart and Winston. All rights reserved.

Name _____ Date _____ Class _____

Famous Rock Groups, continued

5. Sprinkle one type of chip shavings to one side of the crease in the foil within a 4 × 4 cm square. Pat the shavings to make an even layer, and use the edge of the knife to scrape the shavings into the square. Be careful not to tear or cut the foil.

6. Repeat step 4 with the other three types of shavings, making layers of each flavor on top of the previous layer of shavings. Each layer represents a layer of sediment.

7. Fold the top half of the foil over the chip layers. Place this foil package between two heavy books, and apply light pressure for 2 seconds. Remove the foil package from the books, and open the package.

8. What has occurred?
The separate layers of candy chips have been compressed.

9. What kind of rock formation did this simulate?
This simulated a sedimentary rock.

10. What do the books represent in this simulation?
The books represent the newer, upper sediment layers that compress the lower sediment layers with their weight, turning the layers into rock.

11. Place the candy-chip "rock" back in the foil, and put the foil between the two books again. This time, two students should press as hard as possible against the books for one minute. Remove the package from between the books, and open the package.

USEFUL TERMS

mechanical weathering processes that change the physical form of rocks, such as erosion

sedimentary rock rock formed from other rocks as a result of intense heat, pressure, or chemical processes

metamorphic rock rock formed from other rocks as a result of intense heat, pressure, or chemical processes

igneous rock rock formed from cooled and hardened magma (molten rock)

52 HOLT SCIENCE AND TECHNOLOGY

Copyright © by Holt, Rinehart and Winston. All rights reserved.

LABS YOU CAN EAT **133**

Name _____ Date _____ Class _____

Famous Rock Groups, continued

18. Turn off the hot plate, and allow your rock model to cool and harden completely. What type of rock does the cooled candy simulate? Explain your answer.

The cooled candy simulates igneous rock. Igneous rock forms when

solid rock melts and then cools and hardens.

19. Explain two ways the simulation in this lab does not accurately portray the rock cycle that occurs in nature.

Sample answer: In nature the rock cycle requires millions of years to

complete. Also, metamorphic rocks are formed only under condi-

tions of intense heat and pressure.

Teacher's Notes for Going Further:

Consult the geology curriculum at a local college for local geological information as well as common field destinations for college geology classes, such as road cuts. Select a field site, and make sources of information on local geology available to the class before visiting the site. Identify the main types of rocks present to students, and discuss how the rock formations in the area may have been formed.

Going Further

Visit a local area of geologic interest, such as a road cut on a highway, and identify as many different types of rocks as you can. Make a rough sketch of the rocks and the rock formations, and discuss how they might have been formed.

54 HOLT SCIENCE AND TECHNOLOGY

Name _____ Date _____ Class _____

Famous Rock Groups, continued

12. What happened to the layers of chips this time?

The layers of chips fused together.

13. What rock process does this simulate?

This simulates how sedimentary rock changes into metamorphic

rock.

14. What does pushing the books down represent in this simulation?

Pushing the books down represents the intense pressure pushing

on rocks that are deep in the Earth.

15. Now place the aluminum pie plate on the hot plate. Then place the package in the pie plate, and turn on the hot plate. Be sure the package is open slightly at the top so that you can observe what happens.

16. What is happening to the chips?

The chips are melting.

17. What does the hot plate represent?

The hot plate represents the intense heat deep in the Earth that

melts the metamorphic rock after the rock is compressed.

SAFETY ALERT!
- Place the oven mitts on now.
- Do not touch the hot foil package! Be careful working with the hot plate.

LABS YOU CAN EAT **53**

Name _____ Date _____ Class _____

GeoPancakes, continued

HELPFUL HINT
A mug or small bowl with a 10 cm diameter makes a great "cookie cutter" to ensure that your cooked pancakes are all the same size.

5. When you have colored the batter for a pancake, reapply oil and cook the pancake as described in step 3. Then repeat the process until all the pancakes have been cooked, stacking the pancakes in the order in which they were cooked. Allow the pancakes to cool for a few minutes before continuing.

6. Inspect the stack from the side. You have now made a model of a sedimentary rock profile!

Next let's see how changes in the layers affect the appearance of your model.

Formations in the Flapjacks

7. Using the spatula, gently lift the top four pancakes in the stack while a partner removes the bottom pancake. Your partner should then cut the bottom pancake into 10 strips one centimeter wide. Place the strips on their sides, cut side down, next to one another on the plate. The strips of the bottom pancake should now be vertical. Carefully lower the stack of pancakes onto the pancake strips. What kind of geologic formation is represented by this change?

The boundary between the pancake strips and the horizontal pancake

represents an angular unconformity.

8. Explain how this kind of geologic formation might occur in a real rock layer.

An angular unconformity occurs when layers of rock are folded or

tilted and are then covered by a new horizontal layer.

Name _____ Date _____ Class _____

GeoPancakes, continued

9. Remove the fourth pancake (second from the top) from the stack, and tear it in half. Discard one half. Take the remaining half, and scrape it with the fork until it is very thin and has a number of holes in it (the less left of the pancake, the better). Replace the thin pancake half in its original place in the stack.
What kind of geologic formation have you just modeled? Explain.

The thin pancake half represents a disconformity because a part of

the layer is missing from the profile. Disconformities occur when

layers of rock are eroded and then are covered by a new horizontal

layer.

10. Place the chocolate-frosting nozzle between the second and third pancakes. Insert a stream of frosting, moving the nozzle back and forth so that the second pancake is completely covered with frosting.
What kind of geologic formation did you model this time? Explain.

This formation represents a sill. A sill forms when a sheet of magma

flows between layers of rock and hardens.

11. Make a hole in the stack of pancakes by puncturing all but the top pancake layer with a straw. Do not punch through the top pancake. Remove the straw. Place the vanilla-frosting nozzle into the hole, and insert a stream of frosting.
What kind of geologic formation does this represent? Explain.

This formation represents a dike. A dike forms when magma is

forced upward through rock layers and then hardens.

Name _____ Date _____ Class _____

GeoPancakes, continued

SAFETY ALERT!
Be careful when using a knife.

12. While holding the stack of pancakes together, slowly cut the pancake stack in half with a bread knife. In doing so, make sure that you will be able to view all of the formations you have created. Carefully separate the two halves of the stack.

13. Observe the pancake profile you have created. Sketch the profile in the space provided here, and label the geologic layers and features you have represented.

GeoPancakes Rock Profile

Sample answer:

Dike

Disconformity

Angular unconformity

Sill

EARTH SCIENCE ◀◀▶

Name _____ Date _____ Class _____

GeoPancakes, continued

Critical Thinking: Summing Up Your GeoPancake's History

14. A geologist friend of yours sees your geopancake model and exclaims, "Wow! That looks just like a rock profile I saw in the field the other day! Can you tell me how the rock profile formed?" Use your experience of building a geopancake model to write a short narrative describing the history of the rock profile. Be sure to start with the oldest features and to mention as many geologic processes and features as possible, such as deposition, unconformities, erosion, and intrusions.

Sample answer: A layer of sediment was deposited, and then geologic forces caused the layer to fold. Two horizontal layers were deposited on top of the folded layer, forming an angular unconformity.

Another layer was deposited, but wind and water erosion gradually wore away this layer of rock until little or none of the rock remained. The most recent layer was deposited on top of the eroded layer, forming a disconformity. More recently, volcanic activity caused magma to flow between two layers of rock and hardened to form a sill. Finally, magma was forced upward through several layers of sediment and hardened to form a dike.

Answers to Going Further:

A *nonconformity* is a type of unconformity in which stratified rock, such as sedimentary rock, rests on unstratified rock, such as igneous or metamorphic rock. The "geopancakes" batter will spread on the griddle, forming a thin "rock" layer. When these layers are stacked, a "stratified rock" results.

To make a model of an unstratified rock, students should cook the batter in a container that prevents the batter from spreading, such as an egg poacher.

Going Further

A third type of unconformity is a *nonconformity*. Suggest a method of using geopancakes to model this type of unconformity.

Name _____ Date _____ Class _____

Rescue Near the Center of the Earth, continued

Model Analysis Chart

Model layer	Earth layer	Description of Earth layer
Graham-cracker crumbs	Crust	rock, thin layer
Peanut butter mixture	Mantle	moldable, claylike; temperature up to 3,500°C
Jelly	Outer core	molten, liquid; temperature up to 6,000°C
Chocolate chip	Inner core	solid; hottest part of the Earth

Analyze the Results

12. Which layer of the Earth did the team reach by the end of Day 1?

The team reached the mantle by the end of Day 1.

13. Which part of your model represents this layer?

In the model, the peanut butter mixture represents the mantle.

14. On Day 10, the team members continued their journey in the mini-submarine. Describe the layer of the Earth they must have entered in the submarine. How is this layer represented in your model?

The team entered the liquid outer core. They needed the submarine

to travel through the liquid. The liquid outer core is represented by

the jelly.

Name _____ Date _____ Class _____

Rescue Near the Center of the Earth, continued

Draw Conclusions

15. Where will you send the rescue team to look for Dr. Verne and her students? Explain your answer.

I will send the rescue team to the outer core because the team sent

their last report from the outer core.

16. Assume the team is at the place of their last transmission. Was there a layer that the team did not reach? If so, how was it represented on the model? Explain your answer.

The team did not reach the inner core, which is represented by the

chocolate chip. We know this because they never left the submarine

to start digging through the hard inner core.

— Liquid hydrogen
— Liquid metallic hydrogen
— Solid core
— Atmosphere

Going Further

Did you know that the interiors of some other planets in our solar system have a layered structure similar to Earth's? Choose a planet, and find out about its interior structure. Then make a sketch of the planet's structure. Be sure to identify similarities and differences between the planet you chose and Earth.

Answer to Going Further:
Students are likely to find more information about the structure of the inner, rocky planets than the outer, gaseous planets. A sample diagram of Jupiter is provided on this page. If a student chooses to sketch a gaseous planet, such as Jupiter, make sure the student notes the fact that much of the planet is a gas or a liquid instead of a solid.

Name _____ Date _____ Class _____

Cracks in the Hard-Boiled Earth, continued

Egg Sketches

Front view of egg

Rear view of egg

6. What do the cracks in the shell represent?

The cracks represent plate boundaries in the Earth's crust.

7. Describe the patterns created by the cracks in the shell.

Sample answer: The cracks vary in size. Some cracks are isolated,
while others join together or branch apart. Certain parts of the egg
are completely surrounded by cracks.

Name _____ Date _____ Class _____

MAKING MODELS

Cracks in the Hard-Boiled Earth

The Earth's crust is made up of large plates that are in
constant motion. As two adjacent plates move in two
different directions, one of three types of *plate boundaries* is formed: *divergent, convergent,* or *transform*
boundaries. Identifying these plate boundaries helps
scientists better understand the processes occurring in
the Earth. It can also serve a practical purpose, such as
predicting earthquakes.

In this lab, you will use a hard-boiled egg to model
the motion of crustal plates on the Earth's surface.

MATERIALS

- hard-boiled egg
- paper towels
- thin paintbrush
- small bottle of food coloring
- magnifying glass

USEFUL TERMS

convergent boundary
the boundary between
two tectonic plates that
push directly into one
another

divergent boundary
the boundary between
two tectonic plates that
move away from one
another

transform boundary
the boundary between
two tectonic plates that
slide past each other

◀◀ EARTH SCIENCE

Ask a Question

What effects does the movement of crustal plates
have on the Earth's surface?

Conduct an Experiment

SCIENTIFIC METHOD

1. Place the egg on the paper towel, and lightly tap the egg in
different places to produce cracks of various lengths and
sizes. Be careful not to tap too hard.

2. Dip the paintbrush in the food coloring, and trace a number
of the large cracks to make them more visible.

3. Sketch both the front and rear views of the egg in the space
provided on page 68, and show where the cracks are located.
(See the illustration above.)

4. Gently squeeze the egg until slight movement occurs between the pieces of the shell. Use the magnifying glass to
help you see the motion. You should be able to distinguish
at least three types of motion between the pieces of the
shell. Squeeze the egg in different ways to create these types
of motion. Indicate on your sketch the motion of the
eggshell pieces.

Analyze the Results

5. What do the egg and the pieces of shell represent?

The egg represents the Earth. The pieces of shell represent the crustal

plates of the Earth.

Name _____ Date _____ Class _____

Cracks in the Hard-Boiled Earth, continued

8. Describe the three types of motion and their effects on the pattern of cracks.

When a piece of shell moves away from another piece, the crack becomes wider. When a piece of shell moves against another piece, the crack becomes more narrow and the pieces of shell overlap. When a piece of shell moves along a crack, the motion has little effect on the size of the crack.

9. Relate these three types of motions to the three types of plate boundaries mentioned on page 67.

These motions are examples of divergent boundaries, convergent boundaries, and transform boundaries, respectively.

Draw Conclusions

10. Look up the definitions for the following landforms:

- caldera
- volcano
- mountain range
- aquifer
- rift valley
- delta
- strike-slip fault
- cirque

Which of these landforms can be associated with the three types of plate boundaries? Identify the type(s) of motion.

A rift valley can be associated with a widening crack (divergent boundary). A volcano and a mountain range can be associated with a widening or a narrowing crack (divergent and convergent boundary). A strike-slip fault can be associated with side-by-side motion along a crack (transform boundary).

Name _____ Date _____ Class _____

Cracks in the Hard-Boiled Earth, continued

11. What are two weaknesses of using a hard-boiled egg to model the motion of the Earth's crustal plates?

Sample answer: Crustal motion is caused by geologic forces within the Earth, not by the Earth being squeezed. Also, it is difficult to visualize the formation of mountain ranges and subduction zones as one crustal plate slides under another plate.

Answer to Going Further:

Before proceeding with this activity, review the structure of the Earth with the class. Explain to students that the eggshell represents the crust, the egg white represents the mantle, and the egg yolk represents the core. Students are likely to identify a number of strengths and weaknesses in this model. For example, the radius of the Earth's core is a little more than half the radius of the Earth itself, which is similar to the size of the yolk relative to the size of the egg. However, there is an inner solid core and an outer liquid core on Earth that is not distinguished in the model. You may wish to lead a discussion with the class after students have had the opportunity to evaluate the model.

Going Further

You can also use a hard-boiled egg to model the interior structure of the Earth. Using a knife, slice the egg from this activity in two (including the shell), and identify which parts of the Earth the shell, the egg white, and the egg yolk represent. Note at least one strength and one weakness in this model.

Dough Fault of Your Own, continued

18. Holding one piece in place, press and slide the other piece on the tabletop along the direction of the crack. Does the dough slide smoothly as you push or does it stick?

The dough sticks and slides in a jerky motion.

19. How is the rock motion along a transverse fault during an earthquake similar to the motion you modeled in step 18?

The rocks along a fault also stick and slide.

when rocks suddenly unstick and slide.

Rocks on the Slide

20. Remove both parts of Stack B from the freezer. Unwrap the two pieces and place them flat on the table so that the cut ends touch one another. Without allowing the dough to warm, push the two pieces together. The pieces slide against one another. Describe the placement of the two pieces.

One piece is pushed on top of the other.

21. How is the movement of rocks along a reverse or thrust fault similar to this movement?

In a reverse or thrust fault, the rock on one side of the fault is

pushed over the rock on the other side as both rocks are squeezed

together.

Dough Fault of Your Own, continued

◀◀ EARTH SCIENCE

USEFUL TERMS

shortening
the process of moving two spots on the Earth's crust closer together

folding
bending of rock layers made flexible by heat and pressure during shortening

fault
a break between pieces of rock that move relative to one another

transverse or strike-slip fault
a nearly vertical fault in which rock moves both horizontal and parallel to the fault line

reverse fault
an angled fault in which one side of rock is pushed above the other during shortening

9. Stack a light strip on top of a dark strip. Add another dark strip, then add another light strip. You should now have a stack alternating dark and light layers of dough. Set this stack aside.

10. Repeat step 9 twice to make two more stacks.

11. Wrap one stack in a piece of waxed paper, and label it "Stack A." Place Stack A in the freezer for at least 20 minutes.

12. Place another stack on its side so that the alternating colors face upward. Cut the stack in two pieces at a 45° angle to the layers. Wrap each piece in a separate piece of wax paper. Label both pieces "Stack B," and place them in the freezer for at least 20 minutes.

Dough Shortening

13. Place the third stack on a desk or table that touches a wall with one of the short ends flush against the wall. With the base of your palm, compress the dough by pushing the opposite end of the stack toward the wall. What happens to the layers of dough?

The layers of dough fold and buckle but do not break.

14. What geologic process is represented in this model?

This process represents folding.

15. Where would such a process occur? Explain your answer.

Folds are created where rocks are deformed by compressional

forces.

Breaking Even?

16. Remove Stack A from the freezer, and unwrap it.

17. Without allowing the dough to warm, crack the dough against the edge of a table or desk to make two roughly equal pieces. Place both pieces on the wax paper.

Name _____ Date _____ Class _____

Hot Spots, continued

10. Pass the spray can to another student in the group, and re-peat steps 8–9 for the new hole.

11. Continue to repeat step 10. Be sure that every student in the group has a chance to build a whipped-cream mound.

12. After creating whipped-cream mounds over all five holes, pause to observe any changes occurring to the mounds. Then proceed to the discussion questions below.

Analyze the Results

13. What do the holes and the whipped cream represent?

Each hole represents the location of a volcanic island that originally

formed above a hot spot. The whipped cream represents the

magma that flowed upward, fueled by the hot spot beneath the

crust.

14. How did the whipped cream mounds change over time?

Each mound settled after a short period of time, gradually becom-

ing smaller and flatter.

15. What does this suggest about the relative ages of the five Hawaiian islands?

This suggests that the smaller, flatter Hawaiian islands are probably

older than the larger, steeper ones.

Critical Thinking

16. What physical processes might be at work to cause these changes?

Sample answer: Erosion might cause an island to become smaller

and flatter, or the rate of plate motion could have changed over

time as the island was being built up. Also, the weight of the island

could cause it to settle.

Name _____ Date _____ Class _____

Dough Fault of Your Own, continued

◀◀◀ **EARTH SCIENCE**

Critical Thinking

22. If the dough in Stack B were warmed to room temperature, would the pieces of your reverse-fault model be more likely to slide over one another or to bend and fold? Explain your answer.

As the dough becomes softer, the pieces would be more likely to

bend and fold. The pieces would probably stick more as they

warm up and would be less likely to slide.

23. Compare the behavior of the dough as it warms with the behavior of rocks as they are heated.

Just as the dough becomes softer and bends at room temperature,

rocks heated deep in the Earth become more flexible and bend.

Now that you are done with your lab, slice your stacks into cookies! Place the cookies on an ungreased cookie sheet in an oven set at 400°F. Cook for 8–10 minutes.

Meteorite Delight, continued

Meteorite Observation Chart

Trial	Observed		Not observed	
	Meteorite was identified correctly	Meteorite was not identified correctly	Meteorite was identified correctly	Meteorite was not identified correctly
Student 1— Trial 1: plain				
Trial 2: plain				
Trial 3: cocoa				
Trial 4: cocoa				
Student 2— Trial 5: plain				
Trial 6: plain				
Trial 7: cocoa				
Trial 8: cocoa				

6. Switch roles, and repeat steps 1–5. Record the results of all of your observations in the Meteorite Observation Chart.

7. Repeat steps 1–6, except this time the student who is not dropping the balls should NOT observe them dropping. Record your findings in the "Not observed" column of the Meteorite Observation Chart.

Analyzing the Results

8. What did the following parts of the model represent?

  a. plain rice-cereal balls that were dropped

  _____stony meteorites_____

  b. plain rice-cereal balls that were placed on the layer of rice

  _____cereal   earth rocks_____

  c. rice cereal   soil and dirt

  d. cocoa rice-cereal balls   iron meteorites

9. Were your first set of trials representative of meteorite finds or meteorite falls? Explain.

  _____The trials represented meteorite falls because the observer saw the_____

  _____meteorite fall to the ground._____

Hot Spots, continued

Draw Conclusions

17. Which of the five Hawaiian Islands you examined most likely still have active volcanoes? Explain your answer.

  The younger islands (Hawaii, Maui, and Molokai) are most likely to

  have active volcanoes because they are closer to the hot spot that

  generated them.

18. Assume that the Hawaiian hot spot is still active. Is it possible for a new volcano to form another Hawaiian island? Explain your answer.

  Sample answer: Yes. As long as the hot spot is still active, it can still

  propel magma to the surface, forming an underwater volcano that

  may eventually form an island.

19. Identify two weaknesses of using whipped cream to represent the magma that formed the Hawaiian volcanoes.

  Sample answer: One weakness is that whipped cream always re-

  mains soft but magma quickly hardens at the surface. Also, an is-

  land may be flatter than the whipped cream would suggest due to

  weathering and settling.

Going Further

Not all volcanic islands are created by hot spots. Many, like the Aleutian Islands, form over convergent plate boundaries. Others, like Iceland's island of Surtsey, form over divergent plate boundaries. Design an experiment to demonstrate how one of these other types of volcanic islands form.

Answer to Going Further:

Students should recognize that islands formed at convergent and divergent plate boundaries are part of mountain chains in the ocean. The islands are the peaks of the mountains that rise above sea level.
Students should also recognize that an island on a divergent plate boundary is formed from the upwelling of magma similar to the way an island is formed over a hot spot. An island on a convergent plate boundary, however, is formed when the plate itself is lifted as another plate is subducted beneath it.

Name _____ Date _____ Class _____

How Cold Is Ice-Cream Cold? continued

5. What happened to the temperature of the water in the "No Salt" beaker?

The temperature of the water stayed the same.

6. What happened to the temperature of the water with added salt?

The temperature of the water with the salt decreased.

7. Why do you think the salt had this effect on the water?

Accept all reasonable responses.

Make a Prediction

8. If you dissolve salt in ice water, what do you think will happen to the temperature of the water?

Sample answer: The temperature of the ice water will drop after salt

is added.

Conduct an Experiment

9. Divide the cream mixture evenly between two small bags. Force any extra air from each bag as you carefully seal it.

10. Place each cream mixture bag into a second small bag, and seal the second bags.

11. Place one double-bagged cream portion into each of the labeled large bags. The student holding each bag should now put on mittens or gloves.

12. Add 400 mL of ice chips and 100 mL of water to each large bag.

Name _____ Date _____ Class _____

Meteorite Delight, continued

10. Was your second set of trials representative of meteorite finds or meteorite falls? Explain.

The trials represented meteorite finds because the observer did not

see the meteorite fall to the ground.

11. Which kind of meteorite were you more likely to identify correctly? Explain.

The iron meteorites were more likely to be identified correctly be-

cause they appear different than the Earth rocks that were already

on the ground.

12. Other than the appearance of the meteorite, identify another way to determine whether a rock is a meteorite find or an Earth rock. (Hint: Consider what happened to the puffed-rice cereal when you dropped a rice ball.)

The presence of a crater would indicate that the rock is actually a

meteorite.

Critical Thinking

13. Should scientists base their predictions about the number of stony or iron meteorites that exist in outer space on finds or on falls? Explain your reasoning.

Sample answer: Predictions should be based on falls because scien-

tists often cannot identify stony meteorite finds.

Going Further

While a few meteorites are extremely massive and leave craters for scientists to analyze, most meteorites are smaller than a pea. Find out how scientists study these meteorites. Are they more likely to discover tiny meteorites in finds or in falls?

Answer to Going Further

Scientists study tiny meteorites from data collected by satellites. These satellites monitor particles that enter Earth's atmosphere. Thus, scientists are more likely to discover tiny meteorites in falls.

Name _____ Date _____ Class _____

How Cold Is Ice-Cream Cold? continued

Temperature Data Table

Time (min)	Salt		No salt	
	Temperature (°C)	Cream consistency	Temperature (°C)	Cream consistency
0				
5				
10				
15				
20				

23. How did the salt affect the freezing point of water?

The salt lowered the freezing point of water.

Critical Thinking

24. Use your results from step 23 to explain how ice on a sidewalk melts when salt is spread on it, even though the temperature of the ice remains below 0°C, the freezing point of water.

A small amount of ice melts even when the temperature is below freezing, so there's some liquid water for the salt to dissolve in. Since the salt solution has a lower freezing point than water has, the liquid water can't refreeze. Eventually, all the ice melts.

Name _____ Date _____ Class _____

How Cold Is Ice-Cream Cold? continued

13. After 1 minute, measure the temperature of the ice water in each bag by inserting the thermometer bulbs into the water at the bottom of the bags. Record the temperatures in the Temperature Data Table on page 90.

14. Pour the rock salt over the ice in the bag labeled "Salt." Seal both bags carefully.

15. Shake the bags gently for 5 minutes to mix and chill the contents. You may choose to roll the bags back and forth on a desk or tabletop. Be careful not to break the seals on the bags!

16. Carefully open one end of the sealed "No Salt" bag, and insert the thermometer into the water at the bottom of the bag. Record the temperature, and reseal the bag.

17. Repeat the procedure in step 16 for the "Salt" bag.

18. Repeat steps 15–17 twice.

19. Reach into the "Salt" bag, and test the consistency of the cream mixture. If the mixture is still liquid, repeat steps 15–17. If the mixture has begun to solidify, record the temperature and note it as the freezing point in the Data Table. Remove the cream packets from both bags, and place the packets in the freezer to harden.

20. Discard the liquid, salt, and ice in the sink.

Analyze the Results

Look over your results on the chart.

21. What was the lowest temperature reached?

In the bag without salt? 0°C

In the bag with salt? –11°C

22. Was your prediction from step 8 correct? Explain.

Sample answer: No. The temperature dropped to –11°C, which was lower than I predicted.

Copyright © by Holt, Rinehart and Winston. All rights reserved.

Name _____ Date _____ Class _____

LAB 19 STUDENT WORKSHEET

An Iron-ic Cereal Experience

DISCOVERY LAB

You have probably walked down the cereal aisle in a supermarket and seen the phrase "fortified with iron" on many of the boxes. That means iron has been added to the cereal. Have you ever wondered why?

Well, iron helps to carry oxygen to different parts of your body. Green leafy vegetables are great sources of iron, but iron-fortified cereals are too!

How could you find out if there is iron in your cereal? One way you can tell is by using a magnet! Iron is found in two forms: as an element and as part of a compound. Elemental iron is attracted to magnets, while iron in a compound form is not. If the cereal contains elemental iron, the iron can be extracted with the magnet.

MATERIALS
- 2 magnetic stirring rods, each in a small plastic bag
- small amount of iron filings
- 90 g of iron-fortified cereal
- 1 L graduated cylinder
- 500 mL beakers (2)
- water
- 3 dietary iron capsules
- watch or clock

USEFUL TERMS

elemental iron
iron in its pure state

compound
a substance made up of atoms of at least two different elements held together by chemical bonds

SCIENTIFIC METHOD Ask a Question

How can a magnet be used to explore the difference between elemental iron and an iron compound?

Conduct an Experiment

1. Move one of the stirring rods close to the iron filings. What happens?

   The filings stick to the magnet.

2. What does this tell you about the iron in the filings?

   The iron in the filings must be elemental iron.

3. Remove the filings from the outside of the bag, and discard them.

92 HOLT SCIENCE AND TECHNOLOGY

Copyright © by Holt, Rinehart and Winston. All rights reserved.

Name _____ Date _____ Class _____

An Iron-ic Cereal Experience, continued

4. Thoroughly crush the cereal. Place the cereal in the first beaker, and add 100 mL of water. Set the beaker aside.

5. Empty the contents of the iron capsules into the second beaker, and add 100 mL of water. Set the second beaker aside.

6. Roll up the bags containing the stirring rods so that they are easier to hold. After the cereal has become soggy (10–15 minutes), use a stirring rod, magnet side down, to slowly stir the contents of each beaker for 5 minutes.

7. Carefully remove both stirring rods, and examine them closely.

Analyze the Results

8. What did you see on the stirring rod from the first beaker?

   Little black particles were stuck to the stirring rod.

9. What did you see on the stirring rod from the second beaker?

   I didn't see anything on the stirring rod.

Draw Conclusions

10. Based on these observations and what you know about the appearance of iron filings, do you think elemental iron is present in one or both of the beakers? Explain your answer.

   There is elemental iron in the first beaker because the particles on the first stirring rod are dark and metallic, like the iron filings. Also, the particles stick to the magnet. There is no elemental iron in the second beaker.

PHYSICAL SCIENCE

LABS YOU CAN EAT **93**

LABS YOU CAN EAT **145**

Name _____ Date _____ Class _____

Power-Packed Peanuts, continued

Temperature Chart

Water temperature before heating:	_____ °C
Water temperature after heating:	_____ °C
Temperature increase:	_____ °C

Analyze the Results

5. Calculate the energy in the peanut, measured in joules, by calculating the energy absorbed by the water. Use the following formula:

joules = mass of the water × temperature increase × 4.2 J/(g°C)

Show your work.

The amount of joules in the peanut = 100g × 25°C × 4.2 J/(g°C) =

10,500 J (joules).

_____

_____

Critical Thinking

6. Explain why the results obtained from using this apparatus can be inaccurate.

Sample answer: Not all of the heat from the burning peanut reaches the can of water. Some heat is absorbed by the metal in the can, and some heat is lost in the air. The water in the can may be hotter in some places than in others.

_____

_____

_____

Name _____ Date _____ Class _____

An Iron-ic Cereal Experience, continued

11. **What form of iron was in the capsules? Explain your answer.**

The capsules must contain iron in the form of a compound because

nothing stuck to the magnet.

_____

_____

12. **If you dip a magnetic stirring rod in the cereal and no iron sticks to the rod, does that mean there is no iron in the cereal? Explain your answer.**

No. If iron does not stick to the magnet, it might mean that the iron

is in the form of a compound. Iron as a compound doesn't stick to

magnets.

_____

_____

_____

Answer to Going Further:

The term *fortified* on a nutritional label means that nutrients have been added that were never in the food. One example is the addition of vitamin D to milk. The term *enriched* means that nutrients have been added that were once present in the food. Such nutrients are usually lost as a result of food processing, such as making white bread from whole grains.

Going Further

Find out what the terms *fortified* and *enriched* mean when they appear on nutritional food labels.

Name _____ Date _____ Class _____

Baked Alaska, continued

A Baked Surprise

7. What happened to the ice cream on each of the pieces of cake?

The ice cream covered with meringue stayed frozen. The ice cream

that was not covered with meringue melted.

_____

_____

8. Why do you think this happened?

The meringue insulated the ice cream from the heat.

_____

_____

9. Why was it important to make sure that the scoop of ice cream was completely covered with the meringue?

Holes in the meringue would allow heat to reach the ice cream, and

the ice cream would melt.

_____

_____

Answer to Going Further:

Foods containing a large volume of air and little moisture, such as thickly sliced bread, cake, or puffed-grain cereals provide the best insulation. Meringue fits into this category. Foods with high water, oil, or sugar content are likely to melt and are less effective insulators. Examples of these include whipped cream, nondairy whipped topping, jam, or jelly.

Going Further

You can explore the insulating properties of other foods. Repeat the activity with different toppings on the ice cream. Find out which foods most effectively keep the ice cream frozen. Do you see a pattern? Explain your answer.

Name _____ Date _____ Class _____

Power-Packed Peanuts, continued

Critical Thinking

7. How could the results of the experiment be improved?

Sample answer: The results of the experiment could be improved by

stirring the water constantly and by covering the opening in the can.

_____

_____

8. How would you measure the energy content of milk? Explain your answer.

Sample answer: You can't set fire to milk because the milk contains

water, so you would need to convert the milk into a dried powder

first.

_____

_____

_____

_____

Answer to Going Further:

Energy contents for different nuts are as follows: 6.7 Calories per gram of pecans, 6.4 Calories per gram of walnuts, and 5.7 Calories per gram of sunflower seeds.

Going Further

Use your measuring device to test different nuts, such as pecans, walnuts, and sunflower seeds. How does their energy content compare with that of a peanut?

LAB 24 **STUDENT WORKSHEET**

SKILL BUILDER

How To Fluff a Muffin

How do muffins rise in the morning? Like us, they usually need a little help. But instead of an alarm clock, like we use, they rely on a simple chemical reaction. Sodium bicarbonate (baking soda) and an acid combine to produce carbon dioxide gas. What would happen if you left these ingredients out? If you're not afraid of your experiment "falling flat," go ahead and try it!

SCIENTIFIC METHOD

Ask a Question

What are the effects of combining a base (sodium bicarbonate) with an acid (tartaric acid) in the making of muffins?

Make Observations

1. Measure 3 mL of water in the 10 mL graduated cylinder, and pour the water into a test tube.

2. Add the baking soda to the tube, and swirl the mixture. Describe what you see.

   The baking soda is dissolving.

3. Add the cream of tartar to 3 mL of water in the second test tube, and swirl the mixture. What do you see?

   The cream of tartar dissolves in the water.

4. Now pour the contents of the second tube (tartaric acid) into the first test tube. Describe and explain what happens.

   The liquid fizzes. Gas bubbles form because the acid reacts with the base.

MATERIALS

- 10 mL graduated cylinder
- water
- 2 test tubes, 10-15 mL each
- 1.2 mL ($\frac{1}{4}$ tsp) of baking soda (sodium bicarbonate)
- 0.6 mL ($\frac{1}{8}$ tsp) of cream of tartar (tartaric acid)
- 4 paper muffin liners
- 4 prelabeled muffin supports
- 100 mL beakers (4)
- 25 mL graduated cylinder
- 50 mL beakers (4)
- 4 forks
- microwavable plate
- microwave oven
- 2 oven mitts
- metric ruler

Can You Say Seviche? continued

Day 2: Let's Sea the Results

9. Remove your bowls from the refrigerator, and uncover them.

10. Examine the fish in both bowls. Has the appearance of the fish in either bowl changed since yesterday? Describe any changes that you see.

    Sample answer: Yes. The fish in bowl A is now white and opaque.
    The fish in bowl B has not changed. It is still pink and translucent.

11. Using a different spoon for each sample, try to break the fish pieces apart. Describe the texture of the fish when you do this.

    The fish in bowl A is flaky and breaks easily into pieces. The fish in
    bowl B has not changed. It is still tough and rubbery and does not
    break easily into pieces.

12. Compare the fish in bowls A and B with the bowls of cooked fish your teacher has provided. Which bowl of fish looks most like the heat-cooked fish?

    The fish in bowl A looks most like the cooked fish.

13. What does this tell you about the effect of lime juice on fish?

    The lime juice has actually cooked the fish!

Going Further

Around the world, many foods are prepared using a variety of edible acids. Use pH paper to test different foods in your house for acidity, and predict which substances might be used to "cook" food. Then research the cuisine of other cultures for recipes that employ acid-cooking. Identify the acids used in each recipe.

Answer to Going Further:

Supply students with pH paper to investigate acidic foods at home. Have the class brainstorm to come up with a list of foods they could test.

You may also wish to bring to class a variety of international cookbooks that specialize in particular cuisines. If so, you could organize a food festival in which students cook some of the foods they have investigated and share the results with the rest of the class. Possible foods to research include sauerkraut (Germany) and adobo (the Philippines).

Name _____ Date _____ Class _____

How To Fluff A Muffin, continued

Make a Prediction

5. In steps 1–3, you observed the effects of a chemical reaction involving baking soda, cream of tartar, and water. Now you will mix these three substances in various combinations into muffin batter to see how they affect the baking of muffins. Based on your observations from steps 1–3, predict what you think will happen to the muffins as they are baked.

Sample answer: The muffin with baking soda and cream of tartar will rise because the acid and base will produce bubbles. The other three muffins will not rise.

Conduct an Experiment

6. Number and label each paper muffin liner with the name of one person in your group. Place each liner in a support.

7. Each member of your team should mix one of the four batches given below by following these steps:

- Measure and level 40 mL of dry ingredients in a 50 mL beaker by tapping the beaker lightly on the desk. Pour the ingredients into a 100 mL beaker.
- For batches 1–3 only, measure baking soda and/or cream of tartar and mix with the dry ingredients using a fork.
- Make a well in the center of the dry mixture.
- Measure 22 mL of liquid mix in the 25 mL graduated cylinder, and pour the liquid into the well you made in the dry ingredients.
- Stir only enough to moisten the dry ingredients.
- Measure a beakerful of batter with a 50 mL beaker. Level off the batter by scraping the beaker with a fork, and pour the batter into the corresponding liner. Discard the remaining batter in a designated trash bag.

For each batch:
- 40 mL (2 tbsp + 2 tsp) of dry mix
- 22 mL (1 tbsp + $1\frac{1}{2}$ tsp) of wet mix

To batch #1 add:
- 5 mL (1 tsp) of cream of tartar

Name _____ Date _____ Class _____

How To Fluff A Muffin, continued

To batch #2 add:
- 1.8 mL ($\frac{3}{8}$ tsp) of baking soda

To batch #3 add:
- 5 mL (1 tsp) of cream of tartar
- 1.8 mL ($\frac{3}{8}$ tsp) of baking soda

To batch #4 add:
- no additional ingredients

SAFETY ALERT!

Be sure to wear oven mitts when removing the muffins from the microwave oven.

You are now ready to begin baking.

8. Keep all four samples together. Your teacher will coordinate the baking of the batter samples. Baking will take 1.5 to 2.5 minutes.

9. Once your muffins are baked and have cooled for 5 minutes, collect your group's samples.

10. Record and compare the height of your four muffins in the table below.

Muffin Height Data Chart

Batch	Baking soda	Cream of tartar	Height
1	no	yes	1.2 cm
2	yes	no	1.8 cm
3	yes	yes	2.4 cm
4	no	no	1.2 cm

Analyze the Results

11. Compare your results with your prediction, and explain any differences.

Sample answer: The muffin with cream of tartar and baking soda rose the highest, as predicted. However, I predicted the other muffins would not rise at all, but the muffin with baking soda did rise a little. This could be because the baking soda releases some carbon dioxide gas during cooking, even without the acid.

LAB 25

STUDENT WORKSHEET

MAKING MODELS

Fiber-Optic Fun

Have you ever seen telephone workers installing new telephone cables along the highway? The cables are probably not made of copper wire, which carries electrical energy, but of fine, glass fibers that carry light. As amazing as it seems, long-distance telephone companies transmit conversations in the form of tiny pulses of light.

Telephone companies make use of the process of *total internal reflection* to keep a signal from weakening too rapidly over long distances or from leaking out of the fiber as the signal bounces around in the fiber.

When total internal reflection occurs, the pulses of light traveling along an optical fiber act like stones skipping across the surface of a quiet pond. But instead of eventually falling down into the water the way a stone does, the light is reflected into the air.

In this activity, your teacher will demonstrate how fiber optics are used to transmit telephone conversations. Follow along by answering the questions below.

SCIENTIFIC METHOD

Ask a Question

How does total internal reflection allow fiber optics to transmit telephone conversations?

Collect Data

1. Describe the path of the beam of light.

The beam passed straight through the gelatin and out the other side

without bending.

2. Describe the path and the brightness of the beam after your teacher has moved it slightly.

The beam still goes through the gelatin and out the other side and is

about the same brightness. This time the beam is slightly bent as it

exits the gelatin. Also, a dim beam is reflected back into the gelatin at

the far side.

Fiber-Optic Fun, continued

Make a Prediction

3. What do you think will happen if your teacher continues to move the beam in the same direction?

The reflected beam inside will get brighter, and the exiting beam out-

side will get dimmer.

4. Based on your answer to number 3, what do you think will ultimately happen to the beam?

The beam will stay completely inside the gelatin and will be bright.

Draw Conclusions

5. How does total internal reflection allow fiber optics to transmit telephone conversations?

The sound is changed into light that travels through the phone line

without dimming; it keeps bouncing back and forth like the laser in

the gelatin.

Answer to Going Further:

Total internal reflection is used to transmit telephone messages along optical fibers. These fibers are much thinner than a single human hair. Telephone cables are made of many optical fibers. The optical fibers are made of many smaller glass fibers that are each encased in plastic. Just as gelatin is denser than air, glass is denser than plastic. This makes total internal reflection within the optical fibers possible.

When you talk on the telephone, your voice is converted into an electric signal. At a local telephone station, this signal is changed into a digital code consisting of bits, much like the digital code on a CD. The bits of code are used to trigger a tiny laser. The laser encodes your voice as a series of flashes of infrared light that travel through the glass fiber. When you speak, you leave spaces between words. In the fiber these intervals are filled in with someone else's conversation. In fact, a cable of 12 fibers can carry 50,000 conversations at once!

Going Further

Investigate the structure of fiber-optic cables in greater detail. Questions you may wish to consider include the following:

• What are fiber-optic cables made of?
• How many signals can a fiber-optic cable transmit at one time?
• What is transmitted in a fiber-optic cable? How does this differ from a metal cable?
• In what ways are fiber-optic cables an improvement over metal cables?
